What people are saying about
On the Threshold of Hope

A *survivor of sexual abuse says:*

"If you are a survivor of sexual abuse, you are not alone. You hold in your hands not merely the weight of a single book but also the weight of stories that describe what it felt like to be hurt, afraid, hopeless, abandoned, and lost into the darkness. We who are survivors wrestle with overwhelming grief, anger, confusion, and unanswerable questions.

"After years of working with survivors like you and me, Dr. Langberg understands your suffering and respects your long struggle. However, her hope goes far beyond this because she knows what true healing looks like, and she knows that it is available to you. She speaks truth in the face of lies and will lead you to the Truth, the only source of real healing.

"Reading this book will be hard work. Those of us who have gone before you promise that it is a journey worth any cost. What more can I say? Read this book. Take this step toward your own threshold of hope."

—*Isabelle*

A *counselor says:*

"As a counselor, I can promise that this book will touch your life deeply—whether you are a survivor of sexual abuse or someone who has chosen to walk with a survivor on his or her journey to healing. With sensitivity and in clear language, Dr. Langberg will help you face the 'hellishness' of the experience of sexual abuse—but she will also help you to know the presence and power of the Redeemer.

"Because of Diane's many years of experience with survivors, she knows the trauma they face, and she provides a safe place for them to tell their own story. Through her voice and the voices of survivors, you will understand how abuse damaged the survivor's body, emotions, thinking, relationships, and spirit. But you will also hear hope as these same voices—joined by the voice of Jesus, the Redeemer—describe what healing looks like in each of the damaged areas.

"Diane shows how to find strength to distinguish between the distorted reality of the experience of abuse and the truth that can begin to restore wholeness to people who are damaged to the core of their being. She points to biblical stories of sexual abuse and describes how God feels about abuse. She shows that the enemy of our souls, Satan, is the origin of sexual abuse and that God has sent a Champion to fight a battle that no one person, no counselor, no amount of human care and compassion can fight alone.

"This is a refreshing and deeply satisfying book that will unlock the specifics of the healing process and give profound examples of survivors who have walked the healing journey in extraordinary ways. As I read these pages, I was moved, changed, and given a new sense of hope and trust in the One who bore abuse and suffering so that we can be healed."

—*David Gatewood,* **Supervisor of Counseling Services, Focus on the Family**

A pastor and church leader says:

"As I read this book, I became caught up in the content—emotionally, spiritually, theologically, and intellectually. This book is for this moment. It should have been written long ago, but now we have a book that will aid professionals as well as friends and family members of those who walk the road to healing from the wounds of sexual abuse.

"As a minister, counselor, Christian educator, and a cultural apologist, I believe that this book should be required reading for anyone involved in caring ministry—seminary students, pastors, counselors, youth directors, and lay leaders. It is intense reading that not only offers significant insights into healing from sexual abuse but does so from a sound psychology of relationships cast within a clearly biblical theological mold. Langberg's insights into Scripture open new vistas to those of us involved in ministering to people. *On the Threshold of Hope* is an excellent companion to Diane Langberg's earlier book about abuse, *Counseling Survivors of Sexual Abuse.*"

—*Dr. Charles Dunahoo,* **Director of Christian Education, The Presbyterian Church of America**

On the Threshold of Hope

BOOKS IN THE AACC COUNSELING LIBRARY

Psychology, Theology, and Spirituality in Christian Counseling by Mark R. McMinn, Ph.D.

Counseling Children through the World of Play by Daniel S. Sweeney, Ph.D.

Promoting Change through Brief Therapy in Christian Counseling by Gary J. Oliver, Ph.D., Monte Hasz, Psy.D., and Matthew Richburg, M.A.

Counseling Survivors of Sexual Abuse by Diane Mandt Langberg, Ph.D.

OTHER AACC-TYNDALE BOOKS INCLUDE

Family Shock: Keeping Families Strong in the Midst of Earthshaking Change by Gary R. Collins, Ph.D.

Intimate Allies: Rediscovering God's Design for Marriage and Becoming Soul Mates for Life by Dan B. Allender, Ph.D., and Tremper Longman III, Ph.D.

"Why Did You Do That?" Understand Why Your Family Members Act As They Do by Wm. Lee Carter, Ed.D.

Questions Couples Ask behind Closed Doors: A Christian Counselor Explores the Most Common Conflicts of Marriage by James Osterhaus, Ph.D.

High-Maintenance Relationships: How to Handle Impossible People by Les Parrott III, Ph.D.

Fresh Start: 8 Principles for Starting Over When a Relationship Doesn't Work by Thomas Whiteman, Ph.D. and Randy Petersen

Into Abba's Arms: Finding the Acceptance You've Always Wanted by Sandra D. Wilson, Ph.D.

Simplify Your Life and Get More out of It! by H. Norman Wright, M.A.

Changing Your Child's Heart: Parenting Tools to Change Your Child's Attitude, Not Just Behavior by Steve Sherbondy

On the
THRESHOLD
of
HOPE

Opening the Door to Hope and Healing for Survivors of Sexual Abuse

DIANE MANDT LANGBERG, PH.D.

Tyndale House Publishers, Inc. • Carol Stream, Illinois

The American Association of Christian Counselors is an organization of professional, pastoral, and lay counselors committed to the promotion of excellence and unity in Christian counseling. The AACC provides conferences, software, video and audio resources, two professional journals, and a resource review, as well as other publications and resources. Membership is open to anyone who writes for information: AACC, P. O. Box 739, Forest, VA 24551.

Visit Tyndale's exciting Web site at www.tyndale.com.

TYNDALE and Tyndale's quill logo are registered trademarks of Tyndale House Publishers, Inc.

On the Threshold of Hope

Copyright © 1999 by Diane Mandt Langberg. All rights reserved.

Cover illustration by Julie Chen

Designed by Julie Chen

Edited by Lynn Vanderzalm

Library of Congress Cataloging-in-Publication Data

Langberg, Diane.
   On the threshold of hope : opening the door to hope and healing for survivors of sexual abuse / Diane Mandt Langberg.
     p.   cm. — (AACC counseling library)
   Includes bibliographical references.
   ISBN 978-0-8423-4362-6 (pbk. : alk. paper)
   I. Adult child sexual abuse victims—Pastoral counseling of.   I. Title.   II. Series.
BV4463.5.L38   1999
261.8′3272—dc21   98-48043

Printed in the United States of America

15   14   13   12   11   10   09
12   11   10   9   8   7   6

To the many survivors I have known:
Your lives are a testimony
to the redemptive power of the living Christ.
I am honored to have participated
in his work with you and in you.

CONTENTS

Acknowledgments

IN MY previous book about sexual abuse, I acknowledge that
any book is the work of many people, not just one. That is
even more true for this book because it draws directly and
indirectly on the lives and words of many survivors of sexual
abuse. Every survivor I have known has brought me a story,
or a piece of a story, from which all who read will be blessed.
I have gone to school among you all, and I pray that I have
learned the lessons you teach.

Some of you endured the painful task of digging up your
story one more time so that you could contribute specifically to
this book. I know that that digging cost you a lot. As one survivor wrote, "I didn't think that writing about all this would be
any big deal, but as I started writing, I kept getting blocked,
upset at every memory evoked. I would have to put it down, put
it away, not think, and not write. Often I thought of giving up,
but I believe in what you are doing and desperately hope that the
book will reach people in the Christian community." I am grateful to you all.

Again, I am grateful for that very special group of friends who have prayed daily for me. Their commitment to pray each day, not just when I wrote, has blessed and protected my life in many seen and unseen ways.

My associates have prayed for and with me and have taken time from their busy schedules and their own work with survivors to question, edit, and discuss these pages. Dr. Barbara Shaffer, Dr. Phil Henry, Dr. Susan Keortge, Dr. Ruth Palmer, and Elizabeth Hernandez—you continue to delight and challenge me.

Jean Burch, my very gracious and efficient (a rare combination!) office manager, has managed the office and my life, praying faithfully as well.

My editor, Lynn Vanderzalm, is an encouragement professionally and personally. Her prayers, care, and insights are valuable.

Bev Ingelse has continued to mediate my relationship with her computer with humor, grace, and efficiency.

Ron, Josh, and Dan—the three men in my life—continue to demonstrate their commitment to integrity and gentleness. I am grateful for the home you have made together with me.

More important, I have a heart full of gratitude for my Redeemer, who has not only redeemed me but has also blessed me with a taste of the fellowship of his sufferings. That taste has been infinitely precious.

Introduction

THIS is the second book I have written about sexual abuse. The first one, *Counseling Survivors of Sexual Abuse*, was written from the perspective of the therapist's chair. I dealt with what it is like to sit in that chair and what I think therapists need to be and do as they listen to survivors.

This book is written for those who sit in the client's chair. I have listened to survivors in the chair across from me for twenty-five years now, and I have included in this book many of the things they have said and felt and asked. For the most part, my work as a counselor has been with adult survivors of childhood sexual abuse. That means I see adult men and women who were sexually abused before the age of eighteen. I have seen more women than men, although I find more men coming for counseling in recent years.

Some of you who will read this book were raped or sexually abused as adults. You may have been raped by a stranger or by someone you know and love. While this book is not specifically about rape, I believe it will offer you hope and healing because there is much common ground between your experience and the experience of the other survivors who will speak in this book. You will see many similarities in the descriptions of the experience, the damage done to you, and what healing needs to look like.

No matter what your experience of abuse has been, not all of this book will be applicable to all of you. However, it is my hope that as you read, you will feel heard, cared for, understood, and taught. Most important, I long for each of you to find hope within these pages. I know with certainty that there is hope for the darkest of stories because the Light of the World has come. His name is Jesus, and he brings life to dead places, forgives sins, and heals the broken and wounded. I pray that you will find him in these pages.

Lightning struck,
Hit, destroyed,
Blackened, to nothingness,
Nerves, receptors, neurons,
The cells, the transmitters, the receptors
Of feelings, of life,
So that a part of me, parts
Died, were left
Blackened, ashes.

And now, quietly, softly, gently,
Persisting, steady, continuous,
Quietly, I perceive you working,
Sometimes, quietly, I come upon you, working
Slowly, steady, steadily
At the things inside,
At the darkness, death, black
Destruction wrought inside
When the fire coursed, through my innards,
When the darkness passed through my veins.
So there he is, quietly, persistently, inside
Fixing the tendrils, receptors, neurons,
Nerve endings, connecting life, cells, again,
Tending and attaching receptors,
Countering gentling tending
Remaking the path of life coursing
That had once been destroyed.
Sometimes, rounding a corner, I come upon him
Quietly working,
And he is always, steadily, there.
Quietly, reconnecting.

—*sirascol, January 29, 1994*
The Lord is good to those who hope in him.

1

Part One
Approaching the Subject of Sexual Abuse

MOST people approach traumatic subjects with mixed feelings. I suspect many of you are ambivalent about reading a book about sexual abuse. I understand that feeling.

Part 1 will help orient you to the topic of sexual abuse as well as to this particular book. I believe you will find that this section will also instill hope. This book is not meant to overwhelm you with the sin and suffering of sexual abuse. Rather, in the midst of that sin and suffering, I pray that the book instills hope for healing and transformation because we know that the Redeemer has come.

Getting Started

The subject of sexual abuse is a difficult one. Most people do not want to think about it or read about it unless they have some compelling reason to do so. You have just picked up a book about the subject, so I assume something has driven you to look at it. It is likely that either you have experienced sexual abuse or you are close to someone who has.

This book has been written for those who have been sexually abused. To a lesser degree it is also for those who have chosen to walk alongside survivors as they struggle to deal with their history. I have been immersed in the topic of sexual abuse for over twenty years as a therapist. Hundreds of men and women have courageously sat across from me, struggling to find the words to tell me what they often have never spoken aloud before. They have come seeking hope and healing. They have brought me their questions, their pain, their rage, and their fear.

The exchange of such things for hope and healing is never an easy one. It is often a hard and costly labor. It is, however, an exchange that will bring life to those who will persevere. I hope that the pages of this book will encourage you in your own battle with darkness, give you hope that the Light Giver has come, and introduce you to a greater measure of his redemptive power in your life.

You will find within these pages a chorus of voices. First, of course, will be mine. My voice is the voice of one who has listened hard for many years. It is the voice of one whose heart cares deeply about the ravages caused by the evil of sexual abuse. It is the voice of one who knows something of the lies abuse instills and who wants to use these pages to tell you the truth over and over. It is also the voice of one who knows the Redeemer and who has been privileged to have what I call a front-row seat to his work of redemption in the lives of many.

The second voice you will hear often in these pages is the voice of survivors. Elie Wiesel, survivor of the Holocaust, has said that one who was not there can never truly understand it. I was not there, and I acknowledge that I do not know from experience what it is like to be abused. I have been there only as a witness to the testimony of others. But *they* have been there, and I believe it is important to let you hear their voices. This book, then, provides a place where survivors can speak for themselves. These are men and women I have known and loved. They are men and women who have my utmost respect. You will find that many of them will help you find words for the unspeakable. They will also give you hope—real hope. They know the depth of the darkness. They have felt the fear.

To varying degrees they have seen the light dawn. Listen to them. They know the way.

If you are a survivor, the third voice I think you will hear will be your own. The sound of your own voice may initially seem strange to you because sexual abuse often has the effect of silencing its victims. I hope that as you read this book, you will find help expressing what you have not had words for and that as a result, your own voice will be added to those that are included in this book.

The fourth voice you will hear in these pages is the voice of the Redeemer. Some of you are afraid he does not exist. At least not for you. Some of you do not want to know him yet. To trust anyone, perhaps most especially a powerful Redeemer, is unimaginable to you. Some of you long to hear his voice and are desperate to know that he speaks to you. He who is called the Man of Sorrows is here, and he is working even in your darkness. Whether or not you know him, whether or not you believe in him, God through Jesus Christ is the one who brings light out of darkness, hope instead of despair. He is the one who can "rebuild the ancient ruins . . . raise up the former devastations, and . . . repair the . . . desolations of many generations" (Isa. 61:4, NASB). Whatever your story is, there is no darkness he cannot banish, no depth he cannot plumb, no devastation he cannot redeem. I know, for I have seen him do it.

As you interact with this chorus of voices, I hope that you will come to know that you are not alone, that others have to some degree walked where you walk. I hope that you will feel understood and that you will sense that there are others who have a grasp on where you have been and what might lie ahead. This book is intended to assure you that the darkness and suffering you have experienced are indeed real. It is also meant to assure you that there is a way out of the darkness, that others have gone before you and now want to lend their voices to encourage you. It is my prayer that this book will enable you to see yourself "on the threshold of hope."

On the Threshold

Let me tell you a story. It is a horrific story, but then most stories about abuse are like that. It is also a true story. The one thing about it that might surprise you is that it is a story found in the Bible. Most survivors, I find, do not think that Scripture has much to say about abuse. In fact, many survivors have had their abusers use Scripture to justify the abuse. Many survivors are surprised at how well this story captures their experience.

The story takes place among the Israelites, after Joshua died and before the Israelites had their own kings. Periodically the Israelites were ruled by judges, but between the time one judge died and another was appointed, no one was in charge. The result was chaos and lawlessness. It was during one of those chaotic periods that this story occurs. (See Judg. 19, *The Living Bible.*)

The story also happens within the borders of the tribe of

Benjamin. This is the tribe Moses blessed by saying, "Let the beloved of the Lord rest secure in him, for he shields him all day long, and the one the Lord loves rests between his shoulders" (Deut. 33:12). Ironically, the abuse occurred within the tribe that was to experience the security and refuge found in God himself. Like the abuse that happens in many families, these events happened in what ought to have been the place of greatest safety. The place that should have offered safety and security was instead a place of abuse and death.

A Levite, a man of the priestly tribe, took a concubine. That simply means that he lived with a woman without marrying her. She, in essence, had all the duties of a wife but none of the privileges. At one point this woman was in some way unfaithful to the Levite, got angry, left him, and returned to her father's house. Four months later the Levite decided to go to the woman's house and take her back with him to his house. After staying at the father's house for several days, the Levite decided that he and the woman needed to get back on the road. They left the father's house fairly late in the day, traveling only as far as the town of Jebus before it began to grow dark. The unprotected countryside was dangerous at night, and the Levite did not want to stay in Jebus because he would not feel safe in a town where no Israelites lived. The Levite and the concubine pressed on until they reached the nearest Benjamite town, Gibeah. They sat in the town square for some time before an old man offered them shelter.

After the old man had fed the travelers, some men of the city came pounding on the old man's door, demanding to have sex with the Levite. The old man felt that it would be wrong to give over his guest, the Levite, to these men, so the old man suggested that the men take his own virgin daughter and the Levite's concubine instead. When the men would not stop their clamoring, the Levite himself finally pushed his concubine out the door. The men from the tribe of Benjamin raped and abused her all night long.

At dawn, when the men let the concubine go, she dragged herself back to the house where the Levite was and fell down at the door. Sometime during those early morning hours, she died, lying at the door of the house with her hands on the threshold. When the Levite opened the door of the house and found her lying there, he merely said, "Well, come on. . . . Let's get going."

What a chilling story! I am certain many of you can identify with some or all of its components. Some of you know what it is like to be abused in the place that should have been a demonstration of the safety and refuge found in God. You know what it means to have those who ought to have protected you instead hand you over in order to save themselves. The Levite was a member of the tribe set apart to offer sacrifices to God on behalf of the people. Instead, he offered up this woman as a sacrifice for himself!

Many of you know literally what it is like to be gang-raped and abused all night long. You know what it feels like to think that night will never end, that morning will never come. Others know what it is like to drag a beaten and battered body somewhere, hoping against hope to find safety and care. You know also the moment of realizing that no one is going to come to your aid. Others of you have heard the door open and heard the response "Well, come on. . . . Let's get going" or "Put the past behind you." Many of you, I am sure, have experienced a "death on the threshold." Your hope has died. Any sense of being loved or safe has died. And although your body has not physically died, you may feel as if you have died on the inside.

I long for this book, and the voices it contains, to change the picture on the threshold. It is my desire that you who hang on, dead inside, will hear in these pages the sound of the door being opened. The voices at the door will not say, "Let's get going." Instead they will say, "Let me help. There is hope. I know. I have been on that threshold."

The survivors whose voices you will hear in this book know that you cannot get up. They know what it is like to be dying on the threshold. It is my prayer that the understanding and the comfort you will hear in these pages will begin to transform the threshold of death into the threshold of hope.

3

How to Care for
Yourself As You Read

If you have been sexually abused, reading this book will
both draw you and repel you. You will be drawn because
somewhere hope may stir in some hidden corner. Perhaps
someone understands. Maybe there is help. Maybe there is a
way out of the pit. You will be repelled because you are afraid,
because hope is dangerous. It has been crushed so many times
that you dare not let the flame be sparked yet again. And the
thought of reading about sexual abuse is terrifying. You use
tremendous amounts of energy to try to forget, keep it away,
pretend it did not happen. Any discussion about the topic will
easily destroy your fragile defenses against memories you long
to leave behind. Knowing this to be so, I would like to make
some suggestions about how to read this book.

When survivors first come to see me in my office, one of
the things we try to establish is how they will care for themselves during the process of counseling. Dealing with a history

of abuse can be overwhelming and even destructive if it is not handled carefully. Stories have to be looked at bit by bit. Feelings have to be expressed and managed little by little. Memories can cause confusion and fear and an inability to function if they are not treated with care. Hearing from other survivors and considering your own history as you read this book could easily overwhelm you and make life difficult for you. What are some ways to protect yourself as you read?

First of all, do not read at night. So much abuse has occurred under the cover of darkness. Many survivors find it difficult to have any sense of safety at night. To read a book that is likely to trigger memories for you is to work against yourself. So read in the daylight hours, even out in the sunshine if possible. It will make it easier to remind yourself that "that was then, and this is now."

Second, read only in small bits. The chapters are short in order to help you do that. However, I encourage you to stop at any point when you have a reaction to what you are reading. Abuse silences people. I want to provide you the opportunity to find your voice and exercise it. If you have a feeling, a thought, or a memory in response to what you have read, then put the book down and give yourself the chance to speak and to process. Perhaps it would help you to write your responses in a notebook as you read the book. Or you can write comments in the margins of this book.

Third, stop when you have had enough. Many of you know what it means to pay no attention to such signals and to drive yourself to finish or endure no matter what. When you were enduring abuse, you did not have the chance to say, "No, I can't do this," or "Stop!" or "This is too much," and be heard. But here you can say those things. If you feel overwhelmed, stop. If you feel afraid, stop and figure out why. Do not push yourself to finish a chapter simply because it is there. In counseling sessions, when a survivor says to me, "Enough!" or "Can we talk about something else for a while?" I find it is crucial to help the person do that. You can do that for yourself as you read.

Fourth, as I mentioned before, write down your thoughts as you read. Scribble in the margins of this book. Write responses to what you read. Tell your story. Struggle on paper with your feelings, thoughts, and questions. If you are not comfortable writing your thoughts, use a tape recorder and talk out your thoughts and feelings. Again, who you were as well as what you thought and felt were irrelevant to the abuser when you were being abused. That is not so here. Interact, respond, speak. I will make suggestions as we go about how to do that.

Fifth, the best way to deal with abuse is in the context of a safe relationship. If possible, find someone who will journey with you as you read. A counselor who has experience in the area of helping survivors would be ideal. A pastor, mentor, or someone who will be trustworthy, safe, and not dictatorial about how you should think or feel could also be helpful. Choose carefully and wisely. If you end up working with someone who knows little about the subject of sexual abuse, then ask the person to read this book and others from the suggested reading list before you proceed.

Sixth, carefully plan constructive ways to care for yourself as you go. Walking or other aerobic exercise is often helpful to survivors when they feel overwhelmed or agitated. Many find great comfort in music. Distraction in the form of movies or light reading or gardening or working with your hands can be very beneficial. The goal of this kind of activity is twofold. I do not want you to fall back on destructive coping mechanisms such as alcohol, drugs, binge eating, or hurting yourself. I also want to help you find ways to keep from reducing your life to the abuse and its pain. As much as possible you need pockets of time where you are distracted, if not restored.

Finally, reading through this book will hurt. You will want to stop. Healing is often a grueling process. You will tell yourself that this is silly, that something that happened so long ago should be no big deal. You will tell yourself you made it up. You will chide yourself to "get a grip." You will run from, minimize, deny, and attempt to ignore the abuse and its aftereffects. You will feel confused, afraid, angry, and sad. And you will be normal.

I hold out to you the hope of healing. I know it is a reality because I have seen it occur in many, many lives. I also know it is a hard and often exhausting struggle. Many survivors feel worse before they get better. As you dismantle coping mechanisms that you constructed to manage the abuse, you will feel vulnerable and out of control. But if you persevere, you will see change, although it may take years. Like the nation of Israel, you who have known great darkness will see a great light. It will be small initially, barely a flicker, but those living in the land of the shadow of death will find that a light has dawned (Isa. 9:2).

You Are a Survivor

You will notice in this book that I refer to those who have been victims of sexual abuse as *survivors*. I have chosen the word deliberately, and the reason for that is crucial to understanding both the impact of sexual abuse and the healing process.

Our word *survive* comes from the Latin word *supervivere*. It literally means "to live above or beyond." To survive means to keep alive against the odds. It suggests the capacity for endurance. A survivor, then, is one who has experienced something extraordinary and yet manages to keep on going. We use the word *survivors* when we refer to the people who endured the Nazi death camps. We use it when we speak of people who have been through a natural disaster such as a flood or typhoon. We use the word to describe those who have endured life-changing and life-shattering events. Surely the rape or molestation of a little boy or girl is such an occurrence! The rape and abuse of any human is shattering.

SEXUAL ABUSE ALTERS PEOPLE'S WORLDS

When people are sexually abused, their lives are changed, shattered. They will never be the same. A woman who was raped when she was young says, "My comfortable childhood in the suburbs was crushed when I was just eight years old. One day I was a happy, vibrant, trusting, outgoing third grader, and then the next day I was different. Though I did not understand it fully at the time, my life would never be the same again."

Another survivor describes how her life changed because of abuse. "When I was frightened, I would run to my father for safety. I longed for a place of comfort when I was afraid. He would take me on his lap and tell me everything would be okay. *But then everything changed.* Instead of sheltering me and protecting me from my fear, my father took advantage of my vulnerability and began to use my body for his sexual pleasure. I reached out for help and comfort . . . and found abuse."

A third survivor expresses how his world was altered by abuse. "When I was in high school, I worked after school to earn spending money. I loved my job, and I loved my boss. Everyone at the job site trusted and respected this guy, and I found that I wanted to be near him so that I could learn to be like him. He was so different from my dad. But then one day he molested and raped me. I was shattered! How could someone I trusted do this?"

It is at moments such as these that one is transformed into a survivor. The person goes from simply living to living against the odds. The person goes from spontaneity to endurance, from carefree to watchful, from trusting to self-protective. People who continue on in unpredictable and unsafe situations such as chronic sexual abuse must draw on tremendous reservoirs of courage, endurance, and strength in order to go on.

The abuse is particularly life altering for small children. They do not realize that the abuse becomes the pivotal event of their lives. They have no way of knowing how different their lives would have been if they had not been abused. Many victims of childhood sexual abuse struggle to survive in isolation. Either children tell no one about the abuse for various reasons, or they tell someone, and the response is unhelpful or damaging. The result is that these children must develop extraordinary capacities in order to go on. Children who are abused are incredibly resourceful. They draw on deep wells of courage, endurance, creativity, strength, and determination.

I have great respect for the survivors I have known over the years. The characteristics they developed to live against the odds will serve them well when they decide to embark on the healing process.

What about you? How has your world been altered by the abuse you suffered? What characteristics have developed in you as the result of your struggle to survive? What has kept you going when you wanted to quit?

SEXUAL ABUSE SHAPES PEOPLE'S LIVES

On the one hand, to be a survivor is to rise above the difficulty, to move on in spite of the pain, to defy the odds. On the other hand, it means living a life that has been profoundly affected by an atrocity. You develop certain thinking patterns to live with the abuse. You create coping mechanisms to manage the horror of it all. The abuse shapes you. Abuse results in a life lived in reaction to, in protection against, in defiance of, a horror you would like to forget.

The fact that you are a survivor is worthy of commendation. You have done what seemed impossible. You have survived what seemed unbearable. Hold your head up.

The fact that you are a survivor also means that unless you face the horror of the abuse and its resulting lies and strategies for living, your life will continue to be directed by that which you most fear and hate. Having endured the unendurable, you can once again do what seems impossible. You can face the darkness of the abuse, the despair it has produced, and watch the light slowly dawn in places you never wanted to revisit.

God wants to bring you relief and redeem you from this darkness. He himself says, in Isaiah chapter 40: "Comfort, comfort my people. . . . Speak tenderly . . . and proclaim . . . that her hard service has been completed." Through this book I would like to be a voice of comfort and hope for you. It is a comfort and hope I can offer with certainty because I know the God of all comfort. Whatever your story, however you have managed to survive, whatever has been done to you or by you, he has delivered, he will deliver, and he will continue to deliver (2 Cor. 1:10). God *has* delivered you—how do you think you survived the unsurvivable? Who gave you the qualities that enabled you to endure? He *will* deliver you—together we can find ways out of the entanglements of the abuse, freedom from the tentacles that still have a hold on you. He *will continue* to deliver you—the promise is that he will finish the work he has begun in you.

Listen to the voice of a survivor as she writes to others: "As one who has begun the journey toward healing, I want to

reach out to you. I want to offer you a hand of hope and love
and to remind you of qualities that have enabled you to
endure. You are brave. You are faced with a history that is
painful. Your bravery will assist you as you enter into new
ways of thinking and living. You are strong. You have survived
a battle against your spirit. Healing takes great resiliency, and
you will need to draw on that over and over when you feel
weary. You are creative. You learned ways to cope with abuse
and perhaps learned to manipulate abusers for respite from the
abuse. Now your creativity will provide you with new ways to
process, evaluate, and think. The work you have chosen to do
will take time and endurance. But you have
already proven yourself to be a person of endurance. May
Jesus, our Savior, be with you as you struggle, fail, and
triumph. Remember, the Rescue has already happened at
Calvary, and as you move forward, tastes of our final healing
will come."

5

One Woman's Story

I think it would be good to tell you the story of one woman's experience of sexual abuse. The reason I believe this might be helpful is that I find many survivors can see and understand more about the experience of sexual abuse and its aftereffects when they hear about it in someone else's life. They are outraged about hearing what happened in another's life. When it is their own experience, they are often quick to brush it off as "no big deal." Somehow I do not think you will say this woman's experience was "no big deal."

This is a true story. I have chosen it for several reasons, which we will consider later. This story concerns the rape of a young teenager, about fifteen years old, by her older brother. I believe it has much to teach us.

Aaron and Tanya's dad is an extremely wealthy man who knows and loves God. Aaron, the man's oldest child, is due to take over his dad's business. Although Aaron and Tanya have the same father, they do not have the same mother. Tanya's full brother, Adam, who also lives with the family, cares a lot for Tanya and is very protective of her.

As Aaron watches his half sister grow up, he becomes enamored with her and allows himself to fantasize about her. Over time he becomes so obsessed with her that he can think of nothing else. Aaron's lust for Tanya grows so strong that it literally makes him sick. When Aaron's cousin, Jon, asks him what is wrong, he tells Jon about his obsession with Tanya. Understanding the power of raging hormones, Jon helps Aaron plan a way to get what he wants out of Tanya.

One day Aaron pretends to be too sick to get out of bed or to eat. Aaron's dad, hearing about his son's behavior, checks on Aaron to see if he can help. Aaron tells his dad that he probably would eat a little if Tanya brought him some of her special bread. The father thinks this is an easy solution and tells Tanya to bake some bread and take it to her sick brother.

Tanya, happy to help Aaron, goes to him without fear or suspicion. Once she enters his room and they are alone, Aaron tosses aside any pretense of sickness or interest in Tanya's bread. He takes the bread and throws it across the room. Tanya is frightened and confused. Aaron grabs Tanya and tries to force her to have sex with him. She pleads with him not to force her. She reminds him that their dad would be horrified if he knew what Aaron was doing. She begs him not to disgrace her. She warns him that people will lose respect for him if he gives in to his passion.

Blind with rage and lust, Aaron hears nothing she says. Her words are meaningless to him. Using his brute strength, Aaron forces Tanya down and rapes her. As soon as he finishes, he turns livid. He acts as if he hates the very sight of her, making her feel as if she is somehow to blame. He screams at her to get up and leave. Again, Tanya pleads with him, telling him that trashing her after what he has done is as bad or worse than the rape. How can he toss her out and make it look to everyone as if she has done something vile to him? How did this get to be her fault? Aaron refuses to listen. He throws Tanya out of his room, loudly slamming and locking his door so that everyone in the house knows something horrible has happened. She knows they will assume she has done something wrong because of how Aaron throws her out.

Tanya can hardly think. Her heart is pounding. Her life has just been destroyed. She is terrified. She leaves the room, shrieking in anguish and ripping at her clothes. She feels as if her body cannot contain her feelings; they are so overwhelming.

Desperate for help, she goes to her brother Adam. Surely his loyalty to her will help her find a way to deal with this. When Adam finds out what has happened, he says to Tanya, "Don't tell anyone. Our family will never recover from the damage this information will create. Never mind. Don't let it upset you." She is stunned! Don't tell? Don't have any feelings about this? Is he crazy? She feels she has no place to turn. What about her dad? He will help.

When Tanya's dad hears what happened, he is furious. His reaction gives Tanya hope. Her father never seems to doubt the truth of her story. He seems to know that Aaron is capable of such a thing. But although her father shows lots of anger, he does nothing. *Nothing.*

The father's passivity destroys Tanya's hope. Somehow, protecting his oldest son and the reputation of the family seems more important to the father than dealing with his son's appalling behavior or his daughter's feelings. Her father acts as if nothing had happened.

Tanya knows then that she is lost and alone. No one cares. She does not matter. What Aaron did to her matters to no one.

Tanya lives out the rest of her life in the shadow of that rape. She becomes numb to her feelings, almost like a walking corpse. She seems to have no will to live. She wastes away physically. Her beauty, her body no longer matter. She learns to hate herself and becomes very self-destructive. Her grief is more than she can bear.

Tanya's story is similar to many of yours. Although she was older and was "only" raped once, her experience carries many elements common to others. She was forced. She had no choice. She was deceived. In a place and in a relationship that should have provided safety for her, she was in great danger. Her voice was silenced. Her words and feelings had absolutely no impact. She was helpless to stop both the rape and the events that happened in response to it. What she needed or wanted did not matter.

Afterward she was blamed. She was humiliated. Those who should have come to her aid left her alone. She was told not to talk about it. She was told not to let it bother her. In essence, the message was, Do not have any feelings about it. Just get on with your life. There were no consequences for her rapist. Her father, a godly man, did nothing. He passed over his son's crime as if it were of little consequence. The implication seemed to be that appearances, reputation, and her father's hopes for the future of his business meant far more to him than she did.

Tanya's response was one of shame and humiliation. She

was stunned by what had happened. She was emotionally numb. She basically sat around in a stupor. She wasted away. Life held nothing for her anymore. The world was an unsafe place. Her joy was gone. She became self-destructive. Why not? She didn't matter anyway.

Those of you who have experienced sexual abuse can, I am sure, identify with many elements of this story. You know what such feelings are like. You know what it means to be violated by another. You know how it feels to be blamed and trashed by the one who has raped you. You know only too well what it is like to be silenced, to be told not to destroy someone's reputation. You know what it is like to go numb. Many of you know the experience of becoming self-destructive. Tanya became an utterly desolate woman—solitary, abandoned by friends, and without hope.

As you read her story, you most likely feel angry. Angry at the brother who deceived her and so effectively destroyed her young life. Angry at the cousin who helped Aaron trap her. Angry at the stupidity of the father, who did not watch out for his daughter. Angry at the father for caring more about *his* plans than about his daughter's well-being. Angry at the brother who told her to keep silent and not be upset. Angry that a life was used up and tossed aside. Who might she have become? What should her life have been like? What was lost to her and to the rest of the world because she was so effectively destroyed?

If you truly grasp the horror of what was done to Tanya, as well as the profound consequences to her life, then you have a glimpse of what sexual abuse can do. If these are the results of the rape of a fifteen-year-old, then how can we expect other-

wise in the life of someone who is repeatedly raped throughout his or her growing-up years?

Why did I choose this story? One reason is already evident. This particular story carries within it several threads
common to many varied experiences of sexual abuse. That
makes it a story with which many people can identify. I hope
that, like the survivors' comments throughout this book, this
story will help many of you not feel so alone.

It also seemed important to choose a true story. This is not
a conglomerate of many different stories. It is one woman's
true story. It actually happened as it was told to you here. This
is not what *could* happen. This is not what it *might* have felt
like. This is what *was*.

Finally, I chose this story because of where I heard it.
When it was first told to me, I didn't really understand all
that it contained. As with any story, the depth of it was not
immediately apparent. I often find in counseling that one
word or one simple phrase can contain worlds of information
if I am listening carefully. If I am not, then I miss a great deal.

When I first heard this story, I did not listen carefully. I
got the facts, but I failed to hear and learn from the experiences of the people involved. Only after several reruns and
extremely careful listening did I begin to grasp what it was
like to be Tanya. It was then that I realized what a wealth of
information was contained in the story of Tanya, and I wanted
to bring some of that wealth to you.

You see, Tanya's story is really the story of a woman named
Tamar. Her story is found in the Old Testament, in 2 Samuel
13:1-22. Tamar was raped by her half brother Amnon, who was
the heir apparent to King David's throne. Her brother Absalom
is the one who told her to be silent and not be upset about it.

He, of course, hated Amnon, and he later murdered him. King David failed to punish either Amnon or Absalom.

Amnon's rape of Tamar was a blatant violation of the Old Testament law (Lev. 18:9-11; 20:17). What Amnon did was deliberate and defiant disobedience of the law of God. That same law demanded death as a penalty. By failing to hold his son accountable, King David, too, failed to obey. The result of all this in Tamar's life was that she "was desolate in her brother Absalom's house" (2 Sam. 13:20, NASB).

How important it is for us to hear this story that God chose to place in his Word. How clearly it teaches us the terrible aftereffects of sexual abuse. Not only does the Word of God make it very clear that sexual abuse is against God, it also vividly portrays for us what the results of such sin can be in the life of a young girl.

However, for us, the story does not end there. God's Word contains truths that Tamar never had the privilege of hearing. The same God who gave us this story says, "Whereas you have been forsaken and hated with no one passing through [what a description of desolation!], I will make you an everlasting pride, a joy" (Isa. 60:15, NASB). *This* God sent the Redeemer, who said he came to "bind up the brokenhearted, to proclaim . . . release from darkness for the prisoners" (Isa. 61:1). *This* God responds to the cry of those who are oppressed by sending them "a Savior and a Champion" (Isa. 19:20, NASB). How Tamar needed to hear such words! How she needed such a Champion!

Let this story from the Word of God affirm your experience. God knows what sexual abuse does. He hates it. He hates it so much that he has sent Jesus to bear in his own body very similar consequences to those that Tamar experienced. In so doing, God offers redemption and healing to all.

Part Two
Dealing with the Abuse

IN THE following chapters we will talk about what it means for you to tell your story—for some of you, maybe for the first time—and we'll discuss what happens after you tell your story. We will examine not only the definitions of some terms that will help you understand what has happened to you but also the impact of trauma on your life. Then we will explore some of the unique dynamics of childhood sexual abuse and some characteristics of families in which abuse occurs. Finally, we will look at the reality behind the scenes of sexual abuse—that the enemy of our souls is himself the origin of sexual abuse and that God has sent you a Champion and a Redeemer.

6

Telling Your Story

I suspect you had many thoughts and feelings as you read through the story in the previous chapter. There were probably particular parts of the story that you identified with more strongly because they remind you of parts of your own story. I also suspect that many of you have never told your own story before, and I encourage you to take the time to do that now.

Let me give you some suggestions before you start. When I ask the people who come to see me in my counseling office to do this, we first try to figure out ways to think about what to say and also ways to stay safe. This is even more crucial for those who have never before spoken about or even given thought to their own story.

First, you need to think of a safe place to write. Is it better for you to be home or outside or in a restaurant? Should someone be with you, or would you rather be alone? If you write at home, should you have the television on or some music to periodically distract you from what you are doing?

Many survivors are not used to thinking about what they prefer or what is comfortable for them. Either they think I am making much ado about nothing, or they simply won't know the answers. Even if you have no idea about how to answer such questions, I would like you to try. Guess, if necessary. The reason is that we are trying to begin some new patterns even now. One of those is learning to hear your own voice articulate what you prefer, what you fear, what alleviates those fears. Abuse shuts us up. God gave you voice. I want to encourage you to exercise yours.

And that leads us to the reason why you should tell your story. I have been struck again and again through the years with the tremendous battle involved for my clients who are trying, often for the first time, to put their stories into words. Their struggle to find words is often slow and terrifying. At the same time there seems to be a drive to give witness to the truth, and it has been very clear that giving voice to their stories and the depth of their suffering has been a major vehicle for healing in their lives.

You will feel great ambivalence about telling your story. To speak the words leads back to the story—the story you are trying to forget. To tell is to return to the horror. The horror results in the tremendous desire/need to deny. To fail to speak is awful. To speak is equally awful because the telling makes the story real.

If you have experienced sexual abuse, you understand this all too well. Most survivors reach a place in life, maybe not until well into adulthood, where they feel compelled to speak. Often the thing that compels them is finding that they can no

longer tolerate the destructive consequences of the abuse.
So the survivor sets out to tell. And yet there is a great barrier
to telling. Words fail. "It is much harder than I thought."
"You won't believe it anyway." "I cannot tell because then
it will seem real, and it will swallow me up."

One woman who struggled hard to tell her story explained
why giving voice to what had happened seemed so difficult
and pointless: "Being silenced began with saying, 'No, I don't
want to' but being forced to do it anyway. Then my abuser
physically silenced me by pushing my face into the pillow.
Sometimes he would strangle me until I fainted. He paid no
attention to my voice. Maybe that is why I didn't tell anyone
about it. My voice was ineffectual. My voice was lost."

I can assure you that although words are woefully inadequate to describe or capture the suffering of sexual abuse,
even in their inadequacy the words will help set you free. And
although it may seem that speaking will only cause that which
you fear to seem so large as to swallow you up, the experience
of fighting silence with words will in time diminish the size
of what you fear. To speak is to open the door and let a ray
of light in. Yes, that light will expose what is terrifying and
ugly. But that light will also enable you to see the way out. To
speak is to tell the truth. Yes, that truth will confront you with
thoughts and feelings you have worked hard to forget. But that
truth will also work to set you free.

Now you have considered a safe place to sit and tell your
story, and you have a reason why you should tell it. What are
some other parameters that survivors have found helpful?
Daytime hours are usually better than nighttime hours.
Specific time slots help contain the emotions that are stirred
up. For example, "I will work on my story Monday, Wednes-

day, and Friday from four to five in the afternoon." Hold to those limits, and when you are finished, go walk, run, drive, or whatever helps you get distance from it.

Do you see all the new patterns this process involves? You are considering what is good and safe for you; the abuse ignored that. You are being called upon to speak the truth; the abuse silenced your voice. You are carefully setting parameters so the memories do not consume all of your life; the abuse was uncontrollable and uncontainable.

Will you be able to follow all of these ideas neatly and have them work just fine? No. Does that mean you will have failed? No. You are pushing against something old and dark and big. Change will come little by little.

You were not created by God to live in silence. We know from the existence of God's Word—both written and living—that it is his nature to speak. You and I are created in the image of a God who speaks. To be made in the image of God is to have a voice and to express ourselves through that voice.

If you have suffered from sexual abuse, one of the results in your life is that you have been shut up. Your voice has been crushed. Fear has made you inarticulate. Perhaps the denial or deafness of others has silenced you. You may be silenced by the threat of rejection, which you are certain will come if you tell the truth. You have known voices that lie, distort, and deceive. In an attempt to survive, you, too, have learned to lie, distort, and deceive. You pretend you are all right when you are dying inside. You say it was no big deal when your insides were ripped apart. You distort the facts to make it seem not so bad. You say, "At least I wasn't killed," when, in fact, you feel dead.

Let me encourage you to speak, to give voice to the truth

of your life. It is indeed a very difficult thing to do. You will, however, find freedom there. Our God is a God of truth and light. Lies are exposed when truth is spoken. Darkness is banished when light is allowed to shine. Telling your story is not an exercise in futility. It is a means to an end. In and of itself, simply telling your story will not bring healing. However, giving voice to the truth of your life so that the light of God can shine in all its spaces *will* bring healing.

You are a man or woman created in the image of God. He is the God who speaks. He has given you voice. The Israelites, in speaking of their bondage to the Egyptians said, "We cried out to the Lord . . . and the Lord heard our voice and saw our misery, toil and oppression. So the Lord brought us out" (Deut. 26:7-8). David said, "The Lord has heard my weeping. The Lord has heard my cry for mercy; the Lord accepts my prayer" (Ps. 6:8-9).

Let your God-given voice join the voices of those who know the experience of oppression, violence, and abuse. It is a frightening step, I know, but as you take it, God will meet you there. He *is* the Redeemer, and he *will* bring you out.

7

What Happens after
You Tell Your Story

I know this will seem hard to believe. I am sixty years old, but I have never told anyone before. My father, well, my father used to drink sometimes. I guess he couldn't help it. He would, he would . . . my father raped me." One day these words came very hesitantly from a woman in my office. She later reflected about that day. "I remember the day I first said those words. They sounded as if I had screamed them. Why was my voice so loud? I was afraid to look up. I didn't want to see your eyes. I waited for the verdict, 'Crazy, as charged.' The abuse started when I was four and ended when I was eighteen. Forty-two years later I spoke about it aloud for the first time. It was like unearthing something dead. I was certain the stench would be unbearable."

The experience of speaking out loud or writing the story of your abuse for the first time will generate all kinds of thoughts and fears. The past may suddenly seem big and unmanageable. You may want to stuff it back into the locked-away place where you kept it, but now it won't seem to go back.

Some of you lived with terrible threats about what would happen if you told. Whether or not the feeling is rational, you may feel certain that your abuser can "tell" that your silence is broken. One woman talked about how confused she felt after speaking about her abuse for the first time: "That week I spent a lot of time trying to understand what had gone on in the counseling office when I told my counselor my story of abuse. I couldn't figure it out. Why had the counselor believed me? I had always been told that no one would believe me, even if I tried to tell. It didn't make sense. Also, my abuser had said he would know just by looking at me if I told anyone. He also warned me that he would kill me if I told. I was in the house with him all week, and he never knew I had told her. I began to question things. If he lied about his being able to tell if I told, was it possible he had lied about other things as well?"

One man said that he thought he would never tell anyone, not his wife, not his best friend. "I had buried within me stories that I thought I would carry to my grave without ever sharing with anyone." Going back on such a decision is a major step for anyone. Shame often descends like a black cloud. A female survivor said the following: "I didn't want to go to my appointment once the counselor knew. My whole being ached—body, soul, and mind. I didn't want to see the look in her eyes. I imagined that she was repulsed by the sight of the slut sitting in front of her. I was sure she would be furious because I had wasted so much of her time when I was nothing but a cheap whore who was too disgusting to talk to. I felt so small and vulnerable."

It is very important to tell your story. It is just as important to write about the thoughts and feelings you have *after* telling your story. How do you feel about yourself? How do you feel about the abuser? What are you afraid will happen to you? Do you feel relieved and afraid all at the same time? Have you done what you decided to do in order to take care of yourself? Take some time to write your responses in your notebook.

One of the things that will be so important as you move through this book is trying to separate out your voice, the abuser's voice, and God's voice. Oftentimes they will seem as if they all run together. Or yours gets completely squashed, and you can't tell the abuser's words from God's.

What is your voice saying? You may hear it say things such as "I am afraid to tell" or "Bad things will happen" or "Others will know I told" or "I will get hurt" or "It's no big deal" or "Why can't I just forget it?" or "I should be over this by now" or "What good will it do?"

What is the abuser's voice saying? You may hear it say things such as "If you tell, I will hurt you" or "I will hurt someone you love" or "No one will believe you" or "You made it up" or "It never happened" or "It was your fault."

What is the voice of the Redeemer saying? Not what you were *told* he would say, not what you *fear* he will say, but what is he *really* saying? He says, "Have nothing to do with the fruitless deeds of darkness, but rather *expose* them" (Eph. 5:11, emphasis added). To tell the truth is to listen to the voice of the Redeemer. He says, "I took up your griefs and carried your sorrows" (Isa. 53:4, author's paraphrase). The voice of the

Redeemer calls you to bring him your griefs and your sorrows. You do so when you tell your story. It's important for you to listen to his words.

David's prayer in Psalm 35:22-27 is a fitting closing to your story:

O LORD, you know all about this.
Do not stay silent.
Don't abandon me now, O Lord.
Wake up! Rise to my defense!
Take up my case, my God and my Lord.
Declare me "not guilty," O LORD my God, for you give justice.
Don't let my enemies laugh about me in my troubles.
Don't let them say, "Look! We have what we wanted!
Now we will eat him {her} alive!"
May those who rejoice at my troubles
be humiliated and disgraced.
May those who triumph over me
be covered with shame and dishonor.
But give great joy to those
who have stood with me in my defense.
Let them continually say, "Great is the LORD,
who enjoys helping his servant."
(NLT, emphasis added)

8

Understanding Some Terminology

A helpful response to any problem depends on having a clear understanding of that problem. In order for healing to take place in your life, you need to understand both the original offense and the ongoing damage in your life. Sexual abuse does damage to the core of a person. It certainly affects the life of the abused child, but it also can leak poison throughout adult life. The impact of such abuse does not "just go away." Because the impact of sexual abuse is profound, it is crucial that we carefully define what it is, consider how common it is, look at possible symptoms, and then define some commonly used terms.

WHAT IS SEXUAL ABUSE?
Sexual abuse occurs whenever a person—child or adult—is sexually exploited by an older or more powerful person for the satisfaction of the abuser's needs. The range of abuse is broad;

it includes verbal, visual, or physical sexual activity that is engaged in without consent. Sexual abuse is a felony in all fifty states.

Verbal sexual abuse can include sexual threats, sexual comments about the person's body, lewd or suggestive comments, and inappropriate discussions. For example, I worked with a man whose mother frequently talked with him in detail about her sexual needs and preferences.

Visual sexual abuse includes exposure to pornography, to any sexually provocative scene (such as viewing intercourse), to exhibitionism, or to voyeurism.

Physical sexual abuse is much broader than intercourse (forced, unforced, or simulated). It includes any touching that is intended to sexually arouse the abuser. It can also include exposure of the victim's body to others.

HOW COMMON IS SEXUAL ABUSE?

Estimates suggest that by age eighteen, one in four women and one in six men will have experienced some form of sexual abuse. Given the tremendous secrecy that still surrounds the subject of sexual abuse, it is certainly likely that such abuse is much more common than is reported.

Sexual abuse is a onetime occurrence for some people and spans all the childhood years for others. The average age of the child when abuse begins is between six and twelve. For some people, all of their childhood memories include sexual abuse.

The majority of abusers of both male and female victims are male. Most perpetrators (abusers) are considerably older than their victims. Some states require an age difference of five years in order for the contact to be classified as sexual abuse. But the age of the perpetrator does *not* determine

whether the victim is harmed by the experience. *Any* unwel-
come sexual experience can do damage, regardless of the age
differences between the perpetrator and the victim.

HOW DOES SEXUAL ABUSE AFFECT PEOPLE?

The severity of a person's reaction to sexual abuse depends on
many factors. Each person is different. Even if you meet someone whose story seems identical to yours, your reactions may
be different because you are a unique person. This is in part
because both the context in which the abuse happens and how
others respond to the abuse seem to be very significant factors.

Research indicates that certain situations of abuse can
cause greater damage than others. Abuse that occurred more
frequently and is of longer duration is potentially more
harmful. The more closely related the abuser is to the victim
and the wider the age difference, the greater the damage. As
a result, children abused by a biological parent often sustain
great damage. Sexual abuse involving penetration of any
kind is considered more harmful. Abuse that was sadistic or
violent is more harmful. Victims who believe they responded
passively or willingly carry greater self-blame. Victims who
experienced sexual arousal during the abuse are often full of
self-loathing. When the victim tells someone about the abuse
and gets either a negative reaction or no help at all, further
damage is done.

One of the major ways victims of sexual abuse cope with
what has happened is by denying it entirely or at least mini-
mizing its impact. That means that if you are a survivor reading through the previous paragraph, you will tend to conclude,
"See, mine wasn't so bad" or "It could have been a lot worse.
What is the matter with me?" If that is your reaction, then you

are silencing your voice. The important thing is not what is a typical response to similar circumstances. The important thing is, What was it (is it) like for *you?* What did *you* experience? What impact did your experience have on *you?*

You will find me saying repeatedly throughout this book that our God is a God of truth. As you begin to deal with your own history of sexual abuse, you will need to do so in truth. That means speaking the truth about what happened to you. It will also mean speaking the truth about your responses to the abuse. Both truths will be difficult to face and to speak. But doing it will lead to freedom.

DEFINITION OF TERMS

Every field of study seems to have its own language. When unchurched people first enter a church community, they find themselves overwhelmed at all the words and references they do not understand. Until they learn some of the language, they feel confused and left out. The area of sexual abuse also has its own vocabulary. There are some specific terms you will encounter in most of the literature on the subject. Let's define some of these terms so you can make sense out of what you read. You will also discover (probably with some relief) that these terms describe and possibly normalize some of your own experiences. In using a couple of these terms with a client of mine years ago, she said, "You mean they have special words for this stuff? Wow! I guess that means I'm not the only one!"

Triggers

A trigger is anything that reminds you of the abuse. The literal definition of the word is "anything that serves as a stimulus and precipitates a reaction." Smells are often triggers. The smell of a certain cologne, sweat, semen, or a musty odor can bring up very vivid memories of what happened to you.

One client wrote, "Certain smells would trigger me and set me off into a memory. For example, the smell of a skunk threw me into a memory of what had happened on the farm. The abuse happened on an evening when there was a strong skunk scent behind our barn. The smell sent me back there, and everything in the present faded away."

Triggers can be things you hear, things you see, a certain kind of touch, or particular locations. *Anything* that causes you to remember the abuse is a trigger.

Flashbacks

A flashback is a kind of memory that is so powerful that it feels as if the present has faded away and you are actually back in the time and place of the abuse. Often you feel the abuse happening all over again. You can hear the sounds, smell the smells, and feel the touch. It can be terrifying and disorienting. It is hard to hear anything in the present. People seem very far away, and those people in the memory seem more real than those in the present.

Flashbacks can occur as the result of a trigger. Flashbacks can also occur in the process of counseling. As you are trying to tell your counselor about what you remember, the room where you are sitting fades away, and instead of feeling like a thirty-six-year-old woman talking about something that happened when you were five, you find yourself feeling five all over again. You may feel your heart rate go up. Your body can curl up and break out into a sweat. Adrenaline is pumped through your system, and your breathing becomes rapid. As the flashback fades and you return to the present, you feel disoriented and confused. You wonder exactly what happened, and you probably feel embarrassed.

Flashbacks are hard, and unfortunately they are not easily cured. Most survivors find that flashbacks lessen in frequency and intensity as they tell their story. Many survivors also find that it is helpful to have a trusted person be with them when flashbacks occur.

Either a counselor or a trusted friend can be taught how you need them to respond when flashbacks happen. I find that many survivors do not want to be touched during a flashback. They often find it helpful and stabilizing to "follow my voice out." That simply means that I continuously talk to them in a low voice, reminding them of where they are in the present and that what they are remembering is not happening now.

The following describes such an experience: "When a memory would hit, I would get totally lost in it. It was as if the present would fade away into a haze and whatever memory was there would return as if it were actually happening at that very moment. I could literally smell the smells, taste the tastes, and feel the physical effects on my body. I found that the voice of the counselor during a memory could help me keep focused and stay in the present. Throughout the memory she would talk to me, calling me to listen to her, to believe what is true—that I was no longer little or back at the farm. She would tell me to stay in the present, to listen to her voice, to stay with her voice. Her voice was not demanding or panicked. It was gentle and controlled. Her voice was often the only thing that would pull me out of a memory, which otherwise might stay with me for hours or days and consume and disorient me so I could not function in my daily life."

Nightmares

Many survivors of sexual abuse have repeated nightmares. Some survivors have occasional nightmares that may be triggered by a memory they had during the day. For other people, nightmares come every night. When this is the case, many survivors say that they avoid going to bed because it simply means being terrified and abused all over again. Some survivors put off going to bed, sleep in places that feel safer (like under the bed), or stay awake until sleep forces itself on them. "I thought I got away from him so he couldn't touch me anymore. Yet every night he gets me again."

Some survivors' nightmares are bits and pieces of the abuse woven into ordinary dreams. Others' nightmares are simply a replaying, night after night, of literal memories.

Like flashbacks, nightmares are not magically cured. Also like flashbacks, nightmares seem to decrease in frequency and intensity as the memories are talked through with a trusted therapist. Facing the memories in the daylight and having the courage to put them into words seem to dispel their hold.

Dissociation

People who are repeatedly traumatized and have no way out have to find some way to cope with the intolerable. Some survivors do so by dissociating or "spacing out." Dissociation is simply a mental and emotional way of removing oneself from the hurtful and dangerous present. There are various ways to dissociate. You can dissociate so that you don't feel the physical sensations in your body. You can dissociate from emotions so you don't have to feel. Or you can disconnect from reality to the point that you are no longer aware of what is happening at all. Some people dissociate in all three ways at once. Survivors talk about feeling as if they have left their bodies and have become part of something in the room. Others feel as if they are watching someone else take the abuse.

One survivor described it this way: "I would start thinking about the wall—what color it was, how hard it was. I would wonder what it would be like to be a wall. Walls don't have feelings. I decided that the safest place on the wall was way up in the corner, so I would make myself go up there and hide in the wall. Then I *was* the wall, and I would watch as that little girl got hurt by her daddy."

One of the dangers of dissociation is that while it enables you to survive the abuse, it also makes it easier for you to get hurt now. If you are removing yourself to an imaginary world or trying to leave your body, it is harder for you to take care of yourself in the present. Like many things, dissociation may be what enabled you to survive and stay sane, but what may have been helpful has now become unhelpful or destructive. We will discuss dissociation again in later chapters.

These vocabulary words simply describe what you may have experienced. We will use them again as we talk about what sexual abuse does to the victim. I think then that these terms will begin to make sense to you, and you will understand more clearly why such things occur.

9

Dealing with Trauma

Sexual abuse is traumatic. Trauma affects us in many
ways. Listen to the voice of this survivor:

*"PTSD—Post-Traumatic Stress Disorder.
Someone finally has put a label on what I am
experiencing.*

*"I was raped by my father for fifteen years.
I never realized that all the stuff that messes up
my life is a result of that. I'm always afraid;
terrified is the better word. I keep getting these
memories of what happened. They come out
of nowhere. I could be sitting in a park on a
beautiful day when all of a sudden the images
of what he did are right there. Then I feel as if
I am six years old again, not twenty-four. It's
as if the whole thing is happening again. The
counselor called it a flashback.*

"I am afraid of men and small spaces. I can't sleep or concentrate. I jump easily and often get furious for no reason at all. I hate my body. I never want to talk about growing up, and I get anxious around children because they remind me of being little.

"I thought I was crazy. But my counselor said I'm not. She said the way I feel is normal for what I lived through. Normal! Imagine that? I never thought anybody would say this was normal for any reason. She also said there's hope. I'm not sure I know what hope feels like. She said it means that somewhere down the road I don't have to live like this. I wonder if she's right?"

WHAT IS TRAUMA?

Many men and women who have been sexually abused suffer from what is known as Post-Traumatic Stress Disorder (PTSD), a condition marked by several criteria. First, people suffering from PTSD have had an exposure to a traumatic event that involved actual or threatened death or injury, during which they experienced panic, horror, and helplessness. Second, they reexperience the trauma in dreams, flashbacks, intrusive memories, or anxiety in situations that remind them of the event. Third, they demonstrate a numbing of emotions and lack of interest in or avoidance of others and the world. Fourth, they experience symptoms of hyperarousal such as insomnia, irritability, anger outbursts, and difficulty concentrating. This list of criteria may describe you. If you have experienced the last three symptoms for at least one month and if they have significantly affected your life, then you qualify for the diagnosis of PTSD.

The word *trauma* comes from the Greek word for wound. PTSD is the result of a wound to your person. A traumatic event is one in which a person's ordinary coping skills are completely overwhelmed and useless. To be sexually abused is traumatic. To be repeatedly abused throughout childhood is even more traumatic. Ongoing sexual abuse shatters every aspect of the person's being—his or her world, self, faith, and future. This is especially true if the abused person is a child. A child is by definition small, vulnerable, and dependent. When big people who were intended to nurture and protect, instead violate and traumatize, a traumatic event has occurred.

One survivor with whom I worked years ago spoke about being in the home of a friend who had a five-year-old daughter. While the two women were talking, the child was out back playing in the yard. During that time two cars collided on the street, and the child witnessed the accident. She came running in the house, absolutely terrified by what she had seen. She went immediately to her mother, who comforted her and rocked her, repeatedly and simply explaining what had happened, reassuring the child that she was safe. My client later learned that the young girl had nightmares for quite a while after the accident. When she was upset, her parents would repeat the above response many times until the little girl finally stabilized.

This event had a profound impact on my client. It opened her mind to the reality of her own experience at the same age. She was repeatedly raped by an uncle, and although her aunt knew about the abuse, she did nothing to protect my client. She was left alone with her fear, her helplessness, and her panic. She had no one to soothe her or reassure her or comfort her. The contrast was startling, and it enabled my client to see the truth that she had suffered repeated trauma with no way of escaping, no rescuer in sight, and no ability to protect herself. It was a turning point in her healing as an adult.

SEXUAL ABUSE CAUSES DEEP WOUNDS

I am aware that many of you have spent years trying to minimize what occurred to you. Even now you may be thinking, *She is making too much of this.* However, as I repeatedly say, our God is a God of truth. Healing *will not* come unless we begin with truth. How can we possibly find appropriate ways to provide healing to any wound if we are not clear and truthful about the nature of the wound to begin with? If you had a stab wound in your stomach, you certainly would not want a surgeon to glance at your bloody shirt and say, "Oh, just a little cut. That's not really too bad. Let's try this Band-Aid." You would want the surgeon to examine the whole wound carefully before announcing a treatment. If you minimize the abuse that was done to you, if you fail to speak truth, you will find that any effort to heal the wound will be inadequate, merely a Band-Aid on a serious wound. I often encourage my clients to continually ask God to expose what is true as we go along—whether that is about the extent of the wound, their ways of handling the wound, their perceptions of themselves, or their beliefs about God. God always answers a prayer for truth—even though it may take time—because it is his nature to reveal truth.

The wounds inflicted by sexual abuse are not surface wounds. They cut deeply. They threaten to destroy your sense of safety, your faith, and your sense of self.

Your world was changed by the abuse you suffered. Your world no longer felt secure. If the abuse was repetitive, then any illusion of security or hope of safety was shattered. Whatever you did to try to stop the abuse proved to be useless. Maybe you tried to be good, bad, pretty, ugly, or smart, hoping that you could stop the abuser. Maybe you tried to hide or to pray. But most of you found that it didn't matter. The abuse happened again and again.

One survivor described her struggle trying to find security: "I tried to be safe. Nothing worked. I would find hiding places in the woods, in the loft, in the attic. He always found me."

Another survivor expressed it this way: "Safety? Safety was falling asleep at night with the covers over my head and my hands hidden underneath, praying Dad wouldn't come. I still sleep that way all these years later."

You may have found that the abuse damaged your faith as well. Perhaps you pleaded with God to make the abuse stop or to keep you safe. Maybe somewhere along the way, you decided that God was powerless or that he didn't care about you. That is not a surprising conclusion, especially if your abuser continually told you that you were a bad person.

Many survivors wrestle with their picture of God. "When my father sexually abused me, I lost my ability to trust him. He would make promises and then not keep them. He would say loving words to me but then abuse me. My inability to trust him also tragically affected my relationship with God. What would make God any different from my father? All I knew was what I had experienced at the hands of my parents, and it was not trustworthy. It left me unable to trust God. Why should I trust him?"

Another survivor expressed it this way: "I had a lot of sideways thinking about God. The Bible says that children must honor their parents so it would be well with them and so that they would live long. I always took that to mean that whatever my parents did, I was responsible. If I didn't do the right thing, then my parents had a God-given right to kill me."

Abuse shatters your sense of self. When you were abused, the people around you communicated that your thoughts and feelings about what was happening were irrelevant. Your words were treated as meaningless. Any expression of truth about yourself had to be hidden away. Your cries that you didn't want to be abused were not heard. Your statements that you were being abused did not matter. Who you truly are was not acknowledged. You were reduced to pretense.

"My efforts to hide the truth from others succeeded. People saw me as a quiet girl, a nice girl, who minded her own business to the point of blending into the scenery. Fearing what others might find out if they *really* got to know me—a dirty, damaged, and unlovely little girl—I deliberately hid who I was. I even deceived myself. I didn't know who I was anymore."

We will say more about the effects of abuse in later chapters, but for now it is important for you to face the seriousness of the abuse that happened to you. I hope that some of what we have discussed here will help you identify your experience or maybe put it into words for the first time. If you have never given any thought to the damage done by your abuse, then you may find this to be a scary process. If you have thought about it and just written yourself off as weird, then perhaps you have a sense of relief as well.

I want to remind you again of the truth of the matter: Sexual abuse is evil, and evil damages human beings. In our endless efforts to make things manageable, we tend to minimize or make light of horrible events. At the same time, we need to be reminded often that the evil and its resulting damage are not the end of the story. There is hope.

The words of the survivors quoted in this chapter reflect much pain and confusion. They give you glimpses into distorted thinking, overwhelming fear, and unanswerable questions. They give you a perspective on how childhood sexual abuse can reverberate throughout life.

However, you will be glad to know that every one of these survivors has moved beyond the experiences related here. These men and women will let you know, as we move along through the book, about the growth in their lives. They will tell you how God has tenderly and with infinite patience reached down into their hearts and lives and has begun to heal their hurts and alter their responses. They will give you glimpses of the beautiful work of our Redeemer.

10

Childhood Abuse

Most of you were children when you suffered sexual abuse. That fact alone has a great impact on how you have dealt with the effects of the abuse.

What does it mean to be a child? Think about it for a minute. Jot down words that come to mind when you hear the word *child.* Here are some words others have suggested: *little, weak, immature, ignorant, dependent, vulnerable, needy, small, innocent, malleable.* If I brought you someone who met the above description and if I expected you as an adult to take care of that person, what kind of relationship would you need to provide for him or her?

Children depend on adults to tell them the truth. Think about it. How do children learn the names of things? How do they know that a tree is a tree and not a dog? An older person tells them. Children need to be able to trust adults to name things correctly. If, when you were very young, your father told you that trees were dogs, wouldn't you have believed him?

Not only do adults help young children name tangible things, adults also name intangible things such as good, bad, right, wrong, and love. What happens to a small, needy, dependent, malleable human being who is told year after year that evil is good and right or that abuse is love? When many survivors were suffering sexual abuse, they heard the following messages from adults whom they trusted:

"This is what all daddies do for their little girls."

"I have to do this because you are so bad."

"You're my daughter. I can do whatever I want. I own you."

"I can't help myself."

The children who heard these messages had no way of knowing that they were not the truth. It is the nature of children to trust adults.

Do you know what God says about those messages? He says, "Woe to those who draw sin along with cords of deceit, and wickedness as with cart ropes. . . . Woe to those who call evil good and good evil, who put darkness for light and light for darkness, who put bitter for sweet and sweet for bitter. . . . Woe to those who . . . deny justice to the innocent" (Isa. 5:18-23).

Children also depend on adults to teach them about relationships. The adult caregivers in children's lives teach them how to conduct themselves in relationships. It's from these adults that children learn to care for others, to eat at the table, to develop intimacy, to communicate, not to interrupt, not to steal. What those adults say—and, perhaps more important, what they do—teaches children on a continual basis. And what does a dependent, largely ignorant, malleable human being learn when Daddy hits Mommy, when children have to eat on the floor, when uncles rape nieces and nephews, and when cursing is the language of choice?

These reflections from adult survivors of childhood sexual abuse illustrate some of what was going through their heads when they were young and subjected to adults who did not tell them or show them the truth.

> *"Eating was a nightmare in our house. Food was one of my father's gods. You had to eat what was there. He always yelled at the table if anyone messed up, and then he smacked your head. My brother always threw up because he was so nervous. We were timed when we ate. If we didn't eat at the right speed, we had to put our hands on the table, and my father would hit us with his belt, doubled over."*

> *"I never heard kind words in my home. My dad cursed God and was vulgar in literally every sentence. I was confused when other adults did not curse."*

> *"Relationships? I assumed everyone was untrustworthy. I could rely only on myself. I made it my goal to be self-sufficient. I constructed a growing self-protective wall that kept others out and kept me safe."*

> *"I became hyperalert in relationships. I learned how to read my mother, my stepfather, and their friends. I would watch constantly. I had to*

*watch and know everything. If I stayed ahead
of them, I might stay a little safer. I still try to
know everything as if somehow that knowledge
will protect me."*

Children also depend on adults to learn about their bodies and
sexual identity. What happens to a small, dependent, vulnerable
human being whose body is used for sex and who is told
that the shame and guilt are entirely his? What happens to a
little girl who never got touched except when she was being
hit or sexually abused?

*"I had two uncles who raped me. I feel so
confused about myself. Why would men rape a
boy? Does that mean I am gay? Do I give off
certain signals? I feel odd around women, yet
I have been very promiscuous, as if somehow the
more women I have sex with, the more likely it
is that I can prove that I am really male."*

*"My mother used to get in bed with me and
fondle me all through my adolescence. I hate her.
I hate women, especially those who are attracted
to me."*

*"I would put myself in danger with men who
would sexually abuse me. I guess I just wanted
some kind of affection, even if it was awful.
I was starving for someone to touch me. I would
try to find some way to have him hug me. It
didn't always work, but sometimes I would get
hugged. Afterward, I would ignore the pain*

between my legs and the shame I felt because
I could still feel his arm around my shoulder."

Children also depend on adults to teach them about competence, self-confidence, creativity, and initiative. But what happens when small, physically immature, not-very-sure-of-themselves human beings are ignored, criticized, called names, and squashed?

> *"I saw myself as ugly, big, awkward, stupid,*
> *and not worthy of being alive. I always thought*
> *about dying. I couldn't see the point of living."*

> *"I never had any goals. I didn't want to live*
> *long enough to achieve them."*

> *"I was always afraid someone would see how*
> *broken I was. Everyone around me was growing*
> *and living. My life was rote. It was filled with*
> *work and maneuvering. Nothing I ever did*
> *was about growing and adding something to*
> *it. My life was always reactionary and self-*
> *preserving."*

> *"There is an interesting relationship between*
> *my passion for music and my abuse. By the time*
> *I was in eighth grade, I was a fairly prodigious*
> *pianist. Enough so that my parents and teacher*
> *felt I should move up to a better instructor. I*
> *began taking lessons from the man who became*
> *the last of my sexual abusers. In ninth grade,*
> *I abruptly quit, never to return until recently.*
> *Could the abuse have something to do with my*

> *years of aversion toward being identified as a
> musician?"*

One of the assignments I frequently give to my clients who
were abused as children is to visit a school playground or a
church nursery or day-care center and watch children who
are the same age they were when they were being abused. I
instruct my clients to take a notebook and record their obser-
vations about those children. What characteristics do they
observe? How do the children act? What do the children
know how to do? What don't they know? What do they need
from their teachers and other adults?

This is usually a powerful exercise. Part of the reason for that
is that survivors think back on their abuse with adult minds.
They consider what happened and how they responded as if the
child they remember could do what they are now capable of
doing as adults. I find that survivors' perceptions of children,
especially of themselves as children, are far from what is realistic.

My clients will say, "I should have stopped him."

And I will say, "Right, he was thirty-four years old and
two hundred pounds. You were four years old and how many
pounds? Of course, you should have stopped him!"

My clients will say, "Well, when I was older, I should have
told him to quit."

I will say, "Of course, after ten years of terror, isolation,
and forced dependency, you should just wake up one morning
free of fear and able to stand up to your abuser."

Such obnoxious responses on my part, coupled with the
experience of observing other children, often begin to shed
light on a confused mind that for years has been full of lies
and unrealistic expectations.

I encourage you to do what my clients have done. Go back to the age when *your* abuse began. Go and observe children of that age. Then go to the library or bookstore and read some books that accurately describe the developmental capabilities of a child that age. Then, in your mind, put *that child* in an environment of abuse and carefully think through your previous expectations and harsh judgments of yourself.

Remember the child who witnessed a car accident and received appropriate and *needed* care. That experience demonstrates clearly a right response to a dependent, frightened child. And finally, add to that the words of our Savior, who deplores the abuse of little ones: "Whoever welcomes a little child like this [Jesus refers to the little child he had drawn to himself] in my name welcomes me. But if anyone causes one of these little ones who believe in me to sin, it would be better for him to have a large millstone hung around his neck and to be drowned in the depths of the sea. . . . See that you do not look down on one of these little ones. For I tell you that their angels in heaven always see the face of my Father in heaven" (Matt. 18:5-6, 10).

11

What Did You
Learn from Your Family?

What kind of family has sexual abuse in it? We saw from the scriptural story of Tamar that sexual abuse can occur in homes of godly leaders and in homes where love is expressed. Many of you, I am sure, have read enough stories in the media to realize that no type of family is exempt from abuse. Sexual abuse has happened in the homes of the rich as well as the poor, the educated as well as the uneducated, the famous as well as the obscure, the powerful as well as the powerless. Consider the following:

> *"We were dirt poor and lived on the other side of the tracks. My father was an alcoholic and was basically known as the town drunk. I think the whole town knew he 'used' his daughters."*

> *"My uncle was a pastor. Everyone loved him and thought he could do no wrong. He had a*

very charismatic personality, and people loved his sermons. No one in town would hear, let alone believe, anything bad about him. He started fondling me when I was about five. Later, he had intercourse with me. He used to laugh when I said I would tell. 'No one will believe you, girl. You go right ahead and try.'"

If we stood these two men—the town drunk and the beloved pastor—next to each other and asked people to predict who was an abuser, most would point to the first and have a very difficult time believing it about the second. The most consistent and frightening feature of perpetrators, in the testimony of both victims and psychologists, is their seeming normality. This is also true about families in which sexual abuse occurs. We can point to some patterns, but we have no way of gathering a clear picture of which families are likely to have sexual abuse occur within them. This is very disturbing to many people. It would be much more comforting if we could easily recognize both abusers and abusive families. The fact that we cannot means it could be anywhere, which is, in fact, the case.

Let's consider two general categories of families: healthy families and unhealthy families.

HEALTHY VERSUS UNHEALTHY FAMILIES

What distinguishes healthy families from unhealthy families? Healthy families respect a child's individuality and development, have a concern for the child's welfare, and set reasonable, age-appropriate rules and expectations within which the child is taught to operate. These rules and expectations are somewhat flexible and change as the child matures. A healthy family operates somewhere between neglecting and abusing the child on one hand and overprotecting and intruding on the child on the other. In other words, they nurture and protect without intruding or suffocating. There is flexibility and independence without neglect or abuse.

An unhealthy family shows little to no respect or empathy for the growing child. The child's individuality is squashed. Rules and expectations are unreasonable and unrelated to the child's stage of development; for example, a five-year-old is expected to cook breakfast every morning for the family. The parents' rules and expectations are applied unpredictably; what is right one day is wrong the next. The family is characterized by criticism and rejection. Teaching and nurturing are not present. Mistakes result in ridicule, rejection, and harsh punishment. The family can be either overprotective and intrusive or neglectful and abusive.

SOME CHARACTERISTICS OF ABUSIVE FAMILIES

We get some glimpses of what an abusive family is like by listening to survivors describe their families:

> *"My mom had fits of rage at Dad or us. The whole neighborhood could hear her. She would scream and curse until she was exhausted. Then Dad would hit her or choke her to shut her up. I always had feelings of terror and panic. My heart would race. Nights were the worst."*

> *"My cousin abused me. I tried to tell my mom. We were 'the ideal family,' and my mother was very concerned about how we looked to other*

people. When I tried to tell her about the abuse, she got very upset. 'The neighbors would think we were trash if they heard you talk like that. I don't ever want to hear anything like that again.' "

"My dad was a deacon. He had a lot of money. The pastor always treated him special. Dad made us sit on the front row every Sunday. The other people in church never knew what he did to me and my little sister."

"I remember thinking about killing my step-father. With all the guns around our home, I knew just how I would do it. He was a horrible, scary, mean man. He was always terrifying us, shooting his guns, screaming at us. I hated him."

"My grandfather messed with me. He always had me get in bed with him and cuddle. He was quiet and gentle. We all loved him, and every-one knew he was just a little 'odd' sometimes. It wasn't a big deal."

It is obvious that families where abuse occurs can appear to be very different from one another. At the same time, we can see some characteristics that are often present in families where sexual abuse occurs or where the abuse is not responded to when perpetrated by a member outside the family. As we discuss these characteristics, think through the dynamics in your own family.

Families in which abuse occurs often have multiple problems.
Those problems can be as varied as alcoholism or other addictions; family secrets and strong denial tendencies; boundary problems; rigid roles; abandonment; and internal chaos. In these families, family loyalty is strong, and the shame and humiliation run deep. Secrets are fiercely kept. Anyone who talks outside the family is punished or disowned. Often these patterns can be seen throughout several generations. For example, in some families, the father, grandfather, and great-grandfather were all alcoholics. Or a family may include several generations of people who had abortions or who gave birth to children out of wedlock. Or sexual abuse itself may be part of a family for several generations.

Families in which abuse occurs are often rigid in their relational patterns. No one is allowed to be different. Punishment is severe for noncompliance or independence. Outside contacts are discouraged, keeping the family isolated. Anyone who is not related is seen as suspect. Rigidity also shows up in role definitions. Girls and women are good for only certain things. Boys and men are good for other things. Every girl has to be taught "her place."

Families in which abuse occurs are confused about individuals' roles. Children are expected to meet the needs of the parents rather than the other way around. As one survivor said, "Everything in our house revolved around Mother and what she wanted. There wasn't room or time for anyone else." In such families, children take care of the parents and often of other children as well. One woman talked about having to cook for the family when she was still too little to see on top of the kitchen counter. Other survivors talk about being told that their new infant brother or sister was theirs to care for (when they themselves were only four or five).

Families in which abuse occurs send destructive messages. Some of these messages are "Don't think," "Don't speak," "Don't feel." Other families were dominated by these rules and messages: "Always be loyal," "Always cover up," "Always make it look good." Children in such families are at high risk for sexual abuse both within and without the family. These children are deprived and desperate for attention. They are vulnerable to any adult who gives them attention, even when abuse is the required trade-off. These children know enough not to risk disclosure. They have been taught to blame themselves. Self-hatred comes easily. These children have learned how to numb their feelings and continue on as if nothing horrible is happening. These children are simply doing what they have been repeatedly taught. Isn't that what children are supposed to do?

It is important to try to understand what lessons your particular family taught you. What were the dominant messages? What were your family's spoken and unspoken rules? What patterns are you repeating in your adult life? What rules are you afraid to break? Write your responses to these questions in your notebook. None of us learned only good things in our families; we all learned bad things too. However, it is important for all of us to articulate what we did learn so that we can begin to consider whether or not what we were taught is, in fact, truth. Until you state what you know, you cannot find out what is a lie and what is the truth. And as long as the lies remain hidden, they will exert a powerful influence over your life.

12

A Look behind the Scenes

You know, from your own experience and from the reading you have done thus far, that things are not always what they seem. You also know that things are not always what people say they are. People call evil, good; they call bitter, sweet. Many survivors are aware of the gap between what was happening behind the scenes in their lives and how their lives appeared to other people. Listen to the voices of these survivors:

> *"Our family was the picture of respectability. Sort of like finding a beautiful white rock. It looks so pretty, but when you pick it up, you find something dead underneath it."*

> *"We always sat on the front row in church. No one ever knew the horror that went on in our home."*

"My uncle was a pastor. Everyone loved him and thought he could do no wrong. If only they knew."

"I was a child in the hands of an adult three times my size. What was I to do? I was paralyzed. He represented strength, moral rightness, and privilege. My mind was terribly confused by the obvious wrongness of what was happening and the obvious rightness—in my child's mind—of the perpetrator."

APPEARANCES AND REALITY

The gap between appearances and reality exists not only because others didn't know or want to know what was happening to you but also because you practiced pretense. You have not only grown up with circumstances similar to those mentioned earlier in this chapter, but you yourself have also practiced pretense. Some of you have cleaned yourselves up after being abused and gone about your day trying to act as if nothing happened. You have been raped and come down to dinner. You went to church and played the part. Many of you continue that today. Your memories torment you. Your nights are frightening. You hate yourself. Yet, if others were to describe you, they would say you were together, competent, and successful. They have no idea about the reality of your history or your present life.

Now, I am not suggesting that you should not have hidden what was happening or that you should share it with the world now. Many of you hid it as children because, frankly, your lives were at stake. Others of you hid the reality for any one of a hundred reasons—fear, feelings of worthlessness, the fact that no one listened when you tried to tell. Many of you keep silent now because you fear the reactions of others and know no safe place to tell. I understand that. And I would not want you to try to talk about sexual abuse anywhere but in a safe relationship.

My point is simply this: Outward appearances are just that and nothing more—outward appearances. Human beings are easily seduced by appearances. When something looks good, we want it. Often we do not stop to ask whether or not it is really good in the truest sense. Families *look* healthy, so we assume they are. People are usually shocked when they hear about battering or sexual abuse in the homes of those who "appeared" good. Who would have thought?

THE EVIL BEHIND THE SCENES OF SEXUAL ABUSE

Not many people would argue that the sexual abuse of a child is good (although a few would). Sexual abuse is a felony in all fifty states. When we find out it is occurring, we say it is wrong. That is certainly true and right, but if we stop there, we are dealing still on a very elementary level. Let's step back to look at the bigger picture, to look behind the scenes at the source of the evil of sexual abuse.

One of the vilest results of sexual abuse is how it deceives and confuses those who are victims, as well as those who are perpetrators or silent witnesses. It deadens the ability to discern good from evil. It confuses the mind so that truth and error get all mixed up. The tentacles of its lies extend throughout generations.

Scripture tells us that God has called us to truth. He *is* truth. And we are to seek truth. We all have been directly or indirectly taught things that are laced with lies. We live our lives based on those lies until God uses some means to expose them and teach us his truth instead. If you have grown up in a home or family system full of lies and deceit, the impact has probably been profound.

Scripture also tells us that God is light. The outcome of his light in our lives is goodness, righteousness, and truth (Eph. 5:8-9). Anything—no matter where we find it—that does not bear such fruit, is not of God. Even more important, lies, deceit, and evil do not come to us just from people who "couldn't help it" or "don't know better" or "didn't mean it" or "were a little drunk" or anything else we might choose to call it. Jesus tells us that lies, deceit, and evil come to us from the enemy of our souls, the father of lies. Listen to what Jesus says about this deceiver: "He was a murderer from the beginning, not holding to the truth, for there is no truth in him. When he lies, he speaks his native language, for he is a liar and the father of lies" (John 8:44).

Let's explore this verse as a way to help us understand the impact of sexual abuse. Jesus is speaking in this passage to religious leaders. On the outside these leaders appeared to be "good guys." They belonged to the nation of God (Israel), and they were the elite within that nation. They had the right genes and the right job. They busily followed the rules. Yet Jesus says their father is the devil himself!

Jesus then goes on to describe how these leaders follow the father of lies. First, Jesus says that they "want to carry out" the enemy's desires. In other words, they do what pleases Satan or what is in accord with what he wants, and Satan is ruled by his lusts. In other words, these are men who do what they want. Conversely, they do not do what pleases God (appearances to the contrary). Keep in mind as we go along that these guys looked really good to everyone else. People honored these leaders. They were considered the ones who were close to God.

Second, Jesus says their father was a murderer from the beginning. Literally, the word translated "murderer" means "manslayer." The fruit of the enemy's actions is death. He is a life destroyer. He brings death wherever he goes. Those things that produce death rather than life come from the enemy of our souls, no matter how they appear or are presented to us.

Third, Jesus says that our enemy is a liar and the father of lies. To be the father of something is to be its place of origin, its author. That means that lies, *any* lies, come from Satan himself, again, no matter how rational, convincing, or good they sound. We are told that he does not hold to the truth *for there is no truth in him.* He is a deceiver and works very hard to make lies look good and sound true. However, *nothing* that comes from him is truth.

Now look at what we've got: lust, death (destruction of life), and lies. Aren't these the core components of sexual abuse? Isn't anyone who is sexually abused or assaulted being dominated by the lusts of another, whether that be the lust for power, the lust for feeling adequate, or the lust for relieving rage at the expense of another? And doesn't anyone who has been sexually abused experience the destruction of life in some way? Sexual abuse attacks your person, your faith, your security, your world, your hope. And doesn't sexual abuse distort the mind with lies so that what is true seems wrong or irrational and what is a lie seems true and right?

Bluntly put, the evil of sexual abuse is hell brought up to the earth's surface. To fight against the ravages of sexual abuse is to face the outworking of hell itself. To undo the destruction of sexual abuse is to expose lies and seek truth. Such work involves trading death for life. It is a work that involves flesh and blood, but it is ultimately a battle against the powers of this dark world and against the spiritual forces of evil (Eph. 6:12). It is a work that will sometimes seem to skirt the abyss of hell.

THE BATTLE WITH EVIL

Why is it so important to understand the evil behind the scenes of sexual abuse? Let's look at four reasons.

First, any of you who have struggled with the aftereffects of sexual abuse in your life have recognized that it is a difficult battle. People may say to you, "It's the past. Forget it. Put it behind you." You may say such things to yourself. Then you find that you can't simply forget it, and you wonder what's wrong with you. Well, the answer is that *nothing* is wrong with you. You can't have the rubbish of the enemy in your life and just put it behind you and have it be all better. Fighting against the enemy of our souls is a battle. A hard one. It is a fight you cannot do alone or quickly. We who know what the Word of God says about evil are often so naïve about its consequences in people's lives. If the battle to fight the aftereffects of sexual abuse feels hard, it's because it is. That's simply the truth of the matter.

Second, this battle is, in part, about truth. Truth is not a little thing. It is a crucial thing because truth is at the core of who God is. Anything that is not true is not of God. That means that when we pretend, minimize, and deny truth, then we are not in the light. Yes, the light exposes. And yes, that can be excruciatingly painful and disruptive. However, to

walk away from truth is to walk away from the light. Part of
being in the truth is calling things by their right names. That
means evil is not "just a little mistake," and lies are not "fudg-
ing." Scripture tells us that truth is of God and that truth sets
us free. That doesn't just mean palatable truth or pretty truth.
Jesus spoke all kinds of disruptive, disturbing, and unpalat-
able truth in the Gospels. They killed him for that. It is not a
popular thing to do. You will not heal from the evil of sexual
abuse by pretending, denying, or lying about it. It is not
possible.

Third, your childhood taught you lessons about the
unseen. You live out your life as a result of those lessons. Some
of those lessons are filled with lies, and you end up attributing
to God what should be attributed only to Satan. Perhaps you
have come to believe that you are worthless, unredeemable
trash. Perhaps you believe that God's character is not good,
that he does not treasure you, that he is not safe. The lessons
you learned taught you about the unseen—but *which* unseen,
evil or truth? It is vital that you understand them correctly.

Fourth, the battle is worse than you thought it would be.
Yes, it is more far-reaching than you had previously understood. This is not simply a battle with your feelings about
your father, mother, grandfather, grandmother, neighbor,
teacher, uncle, aunt, cousin, or brother. It is not just a battle
with yourself and the destructive things you may have done
to cope and survive. Yes, it is a battle with those things. But
it is also a battle with the powers of darkness and the spiritual
forces of evil. And who are you against such forces? Frankly,
no one. You and I are far too little for such a battle. What are
you to do?

Certainly help on the human level is both good and necessary. You need competent and compassionate people to walk alongside you as you struggle with the issues resulting from the sexual abuse. They not only need to be those who understand what sexual abuse does to people, but they also need to be intercessors. You need people who can pray for you when you cannot pray, who will pray with you when you can or want them to, and who know how to call on God when the struggle is fierce. Even that, however, is not enough. You also need a Champion.

A few verses in Isaiah 19 paint a striking picture of the entrance of this Champion right into the devastation of abuse. Isaiah 19:19-20 describes an altar that would be raised up to God within the borders of Egypt, one of Israel's fierce oppressors. That altar would bear witness to the fact that those who had cried out long and hard to God because of their oppressors would be rescued, for God would send them a Savior and a Defender (Champion). Think of it. An altar to God, raised in enemy territory. What a picture for survivors!

You who have been sexually abused have lived with or known an oppressor. Your person, your body has been used as enemy territory. You have perhaps cried out long and hard, thinking heaven was silent and uncaring. But heaven has sent you a Savior and a Champion in the person of Jesus Christ. He, who himself was oppressed and abused, knows what you have experienced. It is he who is big enough to fight the powers of darkness and the forces of evil. It is he whose power is greater than the power of the enemy. It is he who is the Life Giver and the Fountain of truth.

You may have many questions about your Champion, Jesus Christ. You may have little to no understanding of him. In fact, you may be somewhat afraid of him. You can speak

truthfully about such things. In the midst of those struggles,
I want you to hear clearly from me that I know him. I have
seen his work in the lives of survivors who once had no hope.
His redemptive power is without measure. Who else can make
death bring forth life?

Jesus, your Redeemer, speaks truth. His voice can be
trusted. His Word is sure. He is, in his person, the truths that
he teaches. He calls sexual abuse evil. He allowed himself to
be treated in abusive ways, and he submitted himself to death
so that you would know he understands. So, yes, the battle is
huge. Yes, the work of healing is grueling. But your
Redeemer is here, and he is working.

Part Three
What Was Damaged
in the Abuse?

AS WE move through part 3, we will be considering the various areas of the self and what is damaged because of sexual abuse: your body, your emotions, your thinking, your relationships, and your spirit. Much of this will be painful to read, and I remind you to take care of yourself in the process. Each step of caring for yourself—listening to when you have had enough—is a step toward healing. I also want to assure you that you will not be left only with a look at the damage that has been done, for we will also consider what healing in each of these areas might look like (part 4). If reading this section about damage feels overwhelming, perhaps it would be better for you to alternate, for example, between the chapter about damage done to your body (chapter 13) and the chapter about healing for your body (chapter 18) rather than read all the damage chapters first and then all the healing chapters together. Do what is best for you.

I also encourage you to keep your notebook with you as you read these chapters. Write down the responses you are having. Give voice to some of your thoughts and feelings. Take time to answer some of the questions raised in the chapters. If you have a safe person with whom you can share some of your insights and feelings, start to talk about them with this person. Give voice to what you are learning.

13

Abuse Damaged Your Body

S exual abuse damaged your body as well as how you feel about your body. In this chapter we will look at what it means to live in our bodies, the shame and betrayal you feel because of sexual abuse, and some of the lies you may have come to believe about your body. But first, listen to the voices of these survivors:

> *"Does anybody know what it is like to be wanted only for your body parts? Your mind, your heart, your abilities, your interests are irrelevant. Even your body as a whole is unimportant. Only specific parts matter. That is who you are."*

> *"I have hated and destroyed my body. The impulses to attack it are fierce. It is my enemy. If it weren't for my body, I would have been safe."*

"Nobody wants me except for sex. Men, women, it doesn't matter. I don't know what I am doing. I don't know why they think that is all I want. I don't even know if I have a decent mind. I just know that when people meet me, they think I am put there for their use. I never say no."

"I see myself as called to serve men. Tenderness, touch, compassion have never been in my life. I have never been hugged, held, or kissed except in the context of abuse."

WHAT DOES IT MEAN TO LIVE IN YOUR BODY?

Sexual abuse does damage to the body and the way you think about it. The body, then, is an area where healing needs to occur. In order for you to better understand that damage, let's just consider some aspects of what it means to live in a body.

Your body is permanent. You are born with your body, and you die with your body. You take it with you wherever you go. You cannot exchange it for another, as you can clothing or a house or even a relationship. Your body is a permanent part of your temporal life. As long as you exist on this earth, you exist in your particular body. It is inescapable.

To be stuck in a body you hate or fear is torment indeed. To live in a body you believe has utterly betrayed you and continues to do so is terrifying. To live in a body that reminds you of memories that you would just as soon forget is to feel horribly trapped. To be inextricably tied to what you believe is your greatest enemy is a place of horror for many men and women.

Your body gives you a sense of space. To live in a body also
means to have a sense of space. You physically know where you
end and another person begins. If you watch infants, you will
observe how they learn about body space. When babies discover their toes, they have no apparent knowledge that those
toes are attached to the end of their own bodies and that they
can retrieve their toes at will. Initially, infants are simply surprised and delighted when their toes happen to appear on the
horizon. If these children develop in a healthy environment,
they will be taught that their bodies belong to them, that certain parts of their bodies are not to be touched by most people,
and that they have the right and responsibility to say no.

Infants have a very rudimentary knowledge of their bodies. If this is true, what do you suppose happens to children
who grow up having other people use or command their bodies? Where will the sense of space be? How will these children
learn that there are lines others should not cross and that if
they attempt to do so, the appropriate response is no?

This invasion of body space is much broader than touch.
Certainly when an adult fondles a child's genitals or has sex
with that child, it is a massive intrusion of space. However,
the invasion can occur on subtler levels as well. Children
grow up in houses without doors. Others walk in and out at
will. Adults perform sexual acts in front of children or expose
themselves in ways that teach that body space is nonexistent.
Privacy and respect are totally absent.

If children grow up in such an environment, what do you
suppose happens in later years when someone attempts something sexual? These children do not suddenly have an awareness of space, and they do not understand that they have the
right and responsibility to say no. The lessons these children

learned early on are deeply imbedded. They assumed that the space their body inhabits is public property where trespassing is allowed or even encouraged.

You own your body. If you and others do not acknowledge or honor your body space, then you will not develop a sense of ownership. You will not believe that your body is yours for life and that you need to take good care of it. If your space is continually trespassed, then you will have no sense of choice regarding what happens to your body. You probably will develop an attitude of endurance that teaches you to find some way, *any* way, to survive what is occurring, hoping you can outlast it and come out on the other side. It is hard to care for a body from which you feel so disconnected.

Listen as these survivors describe how they felt about their bodies because of what had happened to them:

> *"For as long as I can remember, my father would watch me dress and undress. There were no doors in our house. He would stand in the doorway, leaning up against the doorjamb, and watch. If I tried to hide or cover myself in some way, I was punished. 'Who do you think you are, hiding like that? Some prima donna? You belong to me, and you will do what I say.' "*

> *"I spent my childhood years trying to find ways to keep my body safe. I went to sleep wrapped up, mummylike in my blankets, hoping my father would leave me alone. He never did. He would come in and laugh, telling me that nothing I tried would work, that I was his, and that if he wanted me, he would have me."*

"I still find it hard to feel when people touch me. I spent so many years trying not to feel any body sensations. Sometimes I will suddenly realize someone has a hand on my arm, and I will not have known when they put it there."

"I have had to work very hard to allow anyone to touch me. Even shaking hands was terrifying. I had never known touch that did not hurt. To let someone touch me meant to get hurt. Why would I want to do that? I still remember the first time that someone put an arm around me and that it actually felt good."

SHAME AND BETRAYAL

It is not hard to see how abuse can lead to promiscuity, passivity, and/or self-harm. Thinking you are good only for sex, thinking you have no rights over your own body, and hating your body with a passion are frequent results of sexual abuse. I find in working with survivors that two things seem to feed these feelings. One is a very deep sense of shame. The second is the feeling of betrayal by those who abused you as well as by your own body.

Shame is a very painful feeling that seems to pervade a survivor's sense of self. We tend to feel a sense of shame when we have done something dishonorable *or* when something dishonorable has been done to us. If you think back to your own abuse, I suspect you can recall feeling humiliated and degraded by what happened. Survivors often tell me they feel "trashed." They feel a loss of dignity and a lack of self-respect. It is not a very big jump from feeling trashed to seeing yourself as trash. To feel that way about the body you are stuck in is a horrific dilemma. The very thing you want nothing to do with is something you cannot escape. When we feel shame, we want to hide. How do you hide from your own body?

Betrayal is the second feeling many survivors have. If your abuser was someone you assumed was safe and would take care of you (for example, a parent, a baby-sitter, or a teacher), the abuse will leave you feeling deceived and misled. These people were not faithful to the particular role they were supposed to have had in your life. You may also feel a deep sense of betrayal from people who were silent witnesses to the abuse: a parent who knew about the abuse and did nothing, a bystander who watched you get raped, anyone who had some awareness and turned a blind eye.

Many survivors also feel betrayed by their own bodies. The intensity of feeling surrounding this sense of betrayal is powerful. Many of you feel betrayed by a body that somehow feels as if it "invited" abuse, by a body that feels as if it "seduced" others without your permission. You feel as if your body was labeled in some way that allowed or even invited what you hated. You think maybe your body was right. You think maybe you really did want the abuse and just didn't know it, or maybe your body knew that sex was all you were good for. Somehow your body went places you did not want to go. It is as if your body was unfaithful to your person.

This sense of betrayal is further intensified when survivors felt some kind of pleasure when they were being abused. Perhaps you grew up hungry for touch, and the only time you experienced touch was during the abuse. You longed for the touch and feel betrayed by that longing, thinking it means you wanted the abuse. Some of you experienced orgasms dur-

ing abuse, and the humiliation feels unbearable. How could
your body do such a thing to you? The orgasm felt good; does
that mean you enjoyed being abused? Your body has become
utterly confusing. Your body feels like the ultimate enemy.
Perhaps your abuser knew that you felt pleasure and used the
information to confirm his or her judgments of you: "I told
you that you asked for it. I told you this is what you were
good for."

Listen as these survivors express the impact of the shame
and betrayal on their bodies:

> *"I began to hate not only my parents and my life
> but also my body. It was the ugliest girl's body
> I knew. I tried to ignore it. Who could blame
> me? I made it work hard. I used to hit myself
> with sticks and punch myself. I knew it was
> bad and needed to be punished. I'd let the ants
> bite me. I would hold my breath, hoping I could
> do so until I died. I used to lie in the bathtub,
> under the water, and try to pass out. I'd pinch
> my privates until I cried."*

> *"I learned well. I had sex with anyone I could.
> I knew some of the people, and some of them were
> strangers. I hated myself, but I couldn't stop.
> I never felt anything good, except once. None
> of them loved me or wanted me or my thoughts.
> They just wanted sex. That was, after all,
> what I was for."*

> *"I would put myself in danger with men who
> would sexually abuse me. I would sometimes set*

up things to be hurt again. I just wanted some kind of affection, even if it was awful. I was starving for someone to touch me. I would put up with humiliation, fear, and pain for affection and attention. When a man would put his fingers inside of me, masturbate on me, or make me do something to him, I would try to find some way to have him hug me or touch me nicely. I always wanted him to hug me—just for a second. Afterward, as I would clean myself up, I could ignore the pain between my legs and the shame and fear I felt because I could still feel his arm around my shoulder."

"I spent ages of years hating my body.
Years that yellowed like sheaves of paper,
Tattered at the edges.
It was my body that betrayed me—my body that
Made them treat me that way.
It needed to be punished, deserved to die.
I decided that my body wasn't really me."
—written by Lynn Brookside

LIES ABOUT YOUR BODY

Two things about our relationship to our bodies are profoundly affected by sexual abuse: We learn how to *think* about our bodies, and we learn how to *care* for our bodies. When the way that we think about and care for our bodies is damaged and full of lies, we usually demonstrate some reflection of the abuse in the way we manage our own bodies. Think through

the following lies with me so you can begin to understand
your relationship to your body.

Lie #1: You are only a body and nothing else. Some of you
have believed the lie that your value resides in your body. You
are very focused on your appearance. Your energy is consumed
by watching your weight, by obsessive exercise, by controlling
your appearance. You believe that if your only value is in your
physical body, then it better be good. If it is not, then you are
worthless.

Lie #2: Your body is the enemy. Some of you have believed
the lie that your body is a hateful thing, worthy only of punishment. You bruise it, cut it, burn it, or damage it with
addictions. You hate it. It is ugly, and you want to destroy it.
If the enemy is not destroyed, it may betray you again.

Lie #3: Your body is worthless trash. Some of you have
believed the lie that your body has no value. You desperately
want it to go away and leave you alone. You neglect it, forget
to feed it, or overfeed it. You refuse to look in mirrors because
they remind you of the existence of your body. You don't want
to wash it or dress it up. You have mastered the coping skill of
feeling "out of body" because that is exactly how you prefer to
live. Your body is not worth your care, and even if it were, you
are uncertain what caring for a body means.

Lie #4: Your gender is the problem. Some of you believe the
lie that if only you could cease to be male or female, then you
would be safe. You manage your body either by trying to be
other than what you are or by attempting to be asexual, your
gender somehow hidden away and unknown. You think that
only people who are gendered get abused; therefore, it is best
to be genderless.

It is understandable that you may believe such lies. If people treated you as if you were invisible except for sex, of course you would assume that your value resides in your body. If you were told you were trash and somehow your body "made" the abuse occur, then certainly you would see your body as the enemy, something to be punished.

To live in a body that feels nothing but pain is to want to run away from that body. Since you could not literally leave your body behind, you learned how to live as if you were outside of your body, not feeling the pain. It's easy to believe that if living in your body only hurts, then living outside of your body must be safe. And, of course, it is true that only people who are gendered are abused. It is not true, however, that appearing to be either of the opposite sex or genderless will prevent abuse.

THE TRUTH ABOUT YOUR BODY

So what is the truth about your body? If your body is not your only value, if it is not trash or something to be disposed of, then what is it? How can you learn to live in a body that you have always hated or feared? It is no easy task. The more chronic your abuse and the earlier it began, the more difficult the task of developing a new relationship to your body. Note that I have not said that the task is impossible; I have simply said that it will be difficult.

Let's examine some truths about your body, keeping in mind that this is not a comprehensive list and that this will not automatically make your relationship to your body better. It will give you a place to start, but this is work most of you will need to do in the context of a healthy and safe relationship with someone who understands these issues.

Truth #1: God made your body and said it was good. The

psalmist says, "For you created my inmost being; you knit me together in my mother's womb. I praise you because I am fearfully and wonderfully made; *your works are wonderful,* I know that full well" (Ps. 139:13-14, emphasis added).

Truth #2: God chose to live in a body. God himself condescended to live in a physical body. Jesus Christ became flesh, and in his body he demonstrated for us the character of God himself. No higher compliment has ever been paid to the human body!

Truth #3: God is willing to live in your body. God tells us that when we accept Christ as our Savior, he will come and live in our body, making it his temple. The only qualification for his presence in our body is that we belong to Christ. The apostle Paul reminds us, "Do you not know that your body is a temple of the Holy Spirit, who is in you, whom you have received from God? You are not your own; you were bought at a price. Therefore honor God with your body" (1 Cor. 6:19-20).

In summary, God says that he created your body, that he was willing to take on a physical body, and that he is willing to dwell in yours. What does sexual abuse do to those truths? Does sexual abuse render the Word of God meaningless? If so, then not one of us is safe. We all have to worry about whether or not we have had something happen to us or have done something to cancel out God's Word.

THE TRUTH ABOUT WHAT GOD SAYS
ABOUT PHYSICAL ABUSE

Let's look at God's Word to see if it helps us understand whether or not our bodies are at fault for sexual abuse. Jesus said, *"For out of the heart* come evil thoughts, murder, adultery, sexual immorality, theft, false testimony, slander. *These* are what make a man 'unclean' " (Matt. 15:19-20, emphasis added). Abuse involves evil thoughts, immorality, theft, and false testimony. Jesus says these come from the heart of the one doing them, *not* from the body to which they are being done. The truth is that the things that came out of the heart of your abuser were the things that made him or her unclean. The abuse did not come from you, and it does not make you dirty.

If your abuse occurred when you were a child, it is very easy for you to believe you were at fault. Children are egocentric. That is why they assume responsibility when a parent dies or a divorce occurs. They endow themselves with power over things for which they have no control or responsibility. This sense of responsibility is only exacerbated when an abuser says, "If you weren't so bad, I wouldn't have to do this." That is a normal childhood thought. It is also a lie. Children think many things that are not true. A healthy environment with loving parents who continually teach truth works to correct and mature their thinking. A destructive environment with abusive or silent parents who continually teach lies works to reinforce those lies.

God says that whatever your parents or anyone else taught you or did to you was a manifestation of their own hearts. If they abused you, there was abuse in their hearts. If they were violent to you, there was violence in their hearts. If they robbed you of safety and nurture, there was malice and neglect in their hearts. If they taught you lies, there was deceit in their hearts.

Some of you may be thinking, *That is all well and good for others, but I went after sex. I was promiscuous. I asked for it. I liked it. I have abused others myself. Obviously then my own heart is just*

*as evil as my abuser's heart. What you say may be true for some peo-
ple, but it is not true for me.*

Actually, some of your thinking is accurate. *All* human
hearts are deceitful and wicked (Jer. 17:9). But that truth
does not negate the truth that whatever your abuser did was
a manifestation of your abuser's heart, not yours. What you
have done reveals your own. If you have been abusive or self-
destructive, it helps you see what is in your heart. Some of you
have not fallen into such behavior because your heart is too
full of fear to do any such thing. Others of you have not done
these things because you are proud and self-righteous, needing
to prove yourself better than your abuser.

So we walk away with two truths: What others do reveals
their hearts, not ours; and no matter what is revealed about
our hearts, we all need a Redeemer. Your heart needs redeeming. Your thinking needs redeeming. The way you treat your
body needs redeeming. Nothing your abuser has done relieves
you of this truth. No matter how heinous your abuse was, *you*
need redemption. The rest of the truth is that there is One
who came to redeem, and nothing that has been done to you
or by you renders his redemptive work void.

Do you want to learn a new way, a redeemed way, to
live in and with your body? Determination will not do it.
Pretending you don't need it will be of no avail. A lot of good
advice will not set you free. Jesus Christ, who inhabited a
body like yours, who for your sake allowed others to humiliate
and betray and abuse his body, has died to redeem your heart.
A redeemed heart does not despise the body. A redeemed
heart does not destroy the body. A redeemed heart does not
ignore the body. A redeemed heart struggles to pursue a right
relationship with the body, even knowing that that may take

many years and incredibly hard work. A redeemed heart knows it is bought with a price, and out of love and adoration for the One who did the buying, a redeemed heart spends a lifetime learning how to glorify God in the body.

(If you need to read more about healing for your body before you go on to read the chapter about how abuse damaged your emotions, read chapter 18 next.)

Abuse Damaged Your Emotions

Sexual abuse damaged not only your body but also your emotions. As a result of the abuse done to you, you may feel overwhelming fear, guilt, anger, and grief. Let's listen to the voices of these survivors as they articulate their emotions, and then let's explore four emotions that are most affected by abuse.

> *"How do I feel? Numb, dead. I have deadened myself to an internal pain for which there is no sedative."*
>
> *"Sometimes I would become enraged. I would hate them with every particle of myself. I would wish them dead."*
>
> *"Feelings? Sure I have feelings—hate, rage, fear, shame. I can't bear up under them. I deaden my feelings with alcohol, pot, any*

*substance I can find. That's the only way
I know to keep my feelings under wraps."*

*"I don't remember the last time I cried. I am
not sure I remember how. I am terrified that if
I start, I will never stop."*

*"It's the fear that is unbearable. I cover it
relatively well, I think, but it never goes away.
I am afraid of men, of women, of the dark, of
small spaces, of sleep, of touch. I never relax.
I never feel safe."*

*"My feelings and fears ran my life. I would
become overwhelmed with fear and begin to
shake. I wanted to run. My mouth would
dry out. I would wonder how I could pass for
normal in the middle of a meeting at work."*

*"Abused children's eyes are so sad. They think
sex is normal. So what if you are only nine and
you don't know what that stuff is or what that
smell is or why some things feel good? So what
if other kids got to play and be children?"*

FEAR

When we are abused sexually or physically by someone whom
we are unable to stop, we suffer trauma. We feel utterly helpless. All the ordinary human responses to danger are rendered
useless. We cannot escape, and we cannot effectively fight
back. Whatever we do doesn't help.

The core response to such helplessness is fear. When we
have been traumatized, fear becomes a way of life. The danger

and the terror drive us to protect ourselves. We can do that by withdrawal or hiddenness, by anger or aggression, or by numbing (that is, finding a way to deaden the fear and its accompanying pain).

Trauma causes us to lose the ability to feel and understand without fear. When we experience ourselves as weak, helpless, and dependent or when we find ourselves neglected and/ or damaged, we often become non-sensing and non-feeling. In chapter 13 we discussed how we disconnect from our bodies. It's important to realize that we also disconnect from our emotions. Or perhaps we retain our connection to anger because it is the one feeling that enables us to feel powerful. For the most part, however, the emotional intensity associated with trauma is so powerful that it overwhelms any normal capacity to bear feelings. I had a client who used to talk about her feelings being "too big" for her body. The level of intensity they reached was simply intolerable.

When feelings become intolerable, relief becomes necessary. Some of you have found relief in alcohol or narcotics. Others find respite in compulsive behaviors such as cleaning, exercising, eating, or having sex. One survivor said, "I have tried to escape reality and feelings any way I could—work, sex, relationships, drugs, food." Perhaps some of you have learned how to disconnect (dissociate) so that your feelings of fear and pain have been severed. It is like a self-generated anesthesia. "I learned as a child how to stop feeling. Whenever I felt terrified, I would stare at something in the room until I could no longer feel what was happening to me."

Sometimes survivors learn that an intolerable emotional state can be terminated by jolting the body in some way. They use self-injury to relieve unbearable emotional pain. The reason this "works" is because the body releases its own analgesic when an injury occurs. When pain is inflicted, the body feels relief and calmness. Physical pain seems easier to endure than the overwhelming emotional pain. Physical pain is also a way to feel alive when for the most part you feel dead.

I would suggest that you stop for a while, get your notebook, and list some of the things about which you are afraid. Let your mind run, and jot down whatever comes. Many of you have never felt free or safe enough even to articulate the fact that you were afraid, let alone what you might specifically fear. If it is hard to do, it might help to start with the sentence "I am afraid . . . " and simply repeat it over and over, finishing it with whatever comes to mind. Allow yourself the privilege of speaking the truth about what you fear.

GUILT

Many survivors are plagued with an unbearable sense of guilt. They are convinced that they somehow caused the abuse. Listen to these survivors' voices:

> *"I should have stopped it. I should have run away."*

> *"What was the matter with me? It got to the point that whenever I went away to camp or anywhere guys hung out together some man would have sex with me. It got to the point that I expected it. It felt good in some way."*

> *"If I hadn't gone out that night, it never would have happened. My parents wanted me to stay home. I didn't listen. It is all my fault."*

"Daddy said that my behavior told him I liked what he did. What was I doing to ask for such treatment? Was it really my fault?"

Participation in something that feels wrong or that is explicitly forbidden may have produced in you a deep sense of badness. This is heightened if anything within the context of the abuse was gratifying. The intensity of guilt rises again if you were forced to become an accomplice in any way. One survivor described her guilt this way: "I was silent when my grandfather began abusing my sister. I would often leave her alone when we were with him so he would mess with her rather than with me."

Guilt is complicated further if your abuser was your primary caretaker. In order to preserve the illusion that their parents are safe people, children find it more palatable to see themselves as the evil ones. "I held on tightly to the belief that I was responsible for what my daddy did. It was more terrifying to think that I was trapped for years living unprotected in the same house with an evil man." Such thinking becomes a core piece of the survivor's identity, and the guilt is deep and pervasive.

It can be a long and difficult process to untangle the threads that make up the ball of guilt. None of us is guiltless. When the sense of our own guilty state before God and others gets all twisted up with the lies of abuse, the burden seems overwhelming and unforgivable. I have seen it cripple many survivors.

Again I encourage you to struggle to find words for your guilt. For what have you judged yourself guilty? Take your notebook, and complete this sentence: "I am guilty for. . . ." Or try completing this one: "If only I . . . , then . . . ." You cannot even begin to separate truth from lies regarding your sense of guilt until you first name what you believe your guilt is about. As you think and write, ask God to help you see yourself as he does. Where does your guilt speak truth, and where does it speak lies?

Any guilt that is not based on the Word of God is false guilt. For example, many survivors who were abused as children feel guilty for the abuse, blaming themselves for its occurrence. God says that we are not responsible for another's sin; we are responsible only for our own. Guilt regarding the abuse is false guilt.

On the other hand, true guilt *is* based on the Word of God. No matter what our history has been or how much others have sinned against us, we must all stand before God for our actions and reactions. While survivors are absolutely *not* guilty for the violence perpetrated against them, they are guilty if they choose a promiscuous lifestyle. We often feel guilty for things for which we are not responsible, and we often run from or deny guilt for things for which we are responsible.

A note of hope: There is healing for both false and true guilt. As God transforms our minds by his truth, he corrects our distorted thinking. Freedom comes as our minds are filled with God's truth. When we are truly guilty and have sinned before God, we can find freedom through Christ's death on the cross. *Nothing* is too big or too awful for that cross. There is no sin that the blood of Christ cannot cover.

ANGER

A third emotion you may be struggling with is anger. While anger is not in itself bad, the intensity of the anger you may feel may seem out of control. Listen to the voices of these survivors:

*"I am angry all the time. I am angry at men, I
am angry at women, I am angry at my abuser.
I am angry at God. When people scare me, I
get angry. When people annoy me, I get angry.
When people disappoint me, I get angry."*

*"The rage seems uncontrollable. I want my
abuser to feel what he did to me. I want to hurt
somebody so he will know what it was like."*

*"I hate women. I have spent my life having sex
with as many as possible so they can feel trashed
the way I did when my mother abused me."*

*"I hide my anger well. It comes out cold and
quiet. I try not to let people know about it, all
the while using it to maneuver them."*

*"My anger terrifies me. I do not trust it and do
not want to feel it. Please help me get rid of it."*

Those of you who are aware of feeling anger probably know
that anger can be a positive force: it helps you keep going; it
helps you fight back; it gives you a sense of power. You also
know that your anger can terrify you and lead you places you
did not really want to go. You say things you didn't want to
say and do things you didn't want to do and then feel humiliated and enraged with yourself for not managing better.

Anger is a normal response to abuse, evil, wrongdoing,
and oppression. Anger, in fact, is God's response to such
things. Many of you deny your anger. In fact, you have done
it so well and for so long that you do not feel any anger at all.
Anger that is not dealt with in proper and healthy ways will

come out "sideways." It might show up in destructive ways such as hurting other people or yourself. It might result in an ongoing depression. Rather than feel anger, some people will just become emotionally flat. Sometimes anger is expressed through the body, in what we call psychosomatic ailments, such as headaches or stomach problems. That simply means that the body is speaking for us about what we are feeling and thinking on the inside.

What do you do with your anger? Do you swallow it? Do you have sudden outbursts or tantrums? Do you become depressed? Are you self-destructive? Do you take it out on other people, either overtly or more subtly? Are you afraid of your anger?

Do you know whom you are angry with? Your abuser is an obvious answer, but what about any silent witnesses, yourself, or organizations that failed to help? Take some time to respond to these questions in your notebook.

Many survivors I see do not think they should speak about their anger. They believe it is wrong to do so. Keep in mind that God articulates his anger on many occasions. The truth is that if you were abused, you will have feelings about that. Naming those feelings truthfully is not wrong. You may need some help with your feelings, but naming them is the first step in that direction. You cannot very well seek help for something you refuse to identify or discuss.

GRIEF

The fourth emotion that may overwhelm you is grief. Each of us grieves in different ways. Listen to the voices of these survivors:

"Oh, the grief . . . I cannot bear the grief. Facing the fear, the memories, the anger was awful. But the grief is unbearable. I lost my childhood. I never got parented. My body belonged to countless others. I lost children. I had no sense of choice. What might I have been? I felt no love or intimacy. I am still not sure I know what those words mean."

"The grief comes in waves. The sobbing is exhausting. It makes me throw up."

"How can such things be? Do you know the grief of being raped at age four? The grief of never living in a safe place? The grief of forced abortions? Some days I think it will crush me."

"Loss? I was kidnapped and raped when I was eight years old. I wrote this poem to express my grief:

> *"A child walks out*
> > *unknowing and pure*
> > > *is captured, damaged, gagged, and left alone.*
> *Would she ever see home again?*
> *Could she ever stand straight and tall again?*

> *"No one else knew her secret*
> > *or dared to ask.*
> *Pink and white*
> > *turned to black and filthy.*
> *A great gift*
> > *turned to a dreaded act.*

Her whole life faking it,
making others think
everything is all right."

To face your history means to face your losses. This will result
in grief you have long struggled to avoid. It seems better to
feel afraid or angry. Perhaps you have worked hard to pretend
the abuse did not happen. Or maybe you have minimized it,
making it smaller, more tolerable.

One experience of rape in the life of an adult changes
the color of the world forever. That feeling is only intensified when abuse is chronic throughout childhood. Once any
trauma has occurred, the illusion that the world is safe is
destroyed. Gone forever.

Many survivors tell me they fear their grief. They are sure
they will get lost in it and never come out. A client recently
listed some of her losses: "Growing up, I never had someone
who wanted to hear my thoughts, privacy in the bathroom,
hugs when I cried, a clean mind when I was a child, a true
mommy and daddy (some days I still want one), a sense of
hope, someone to trust. I do not remember a time when I did
not feel like a slut. A kid like this should have died. It would
have been easier and more kind."

Perhaps as you read, you are aware of some of your own
losses and the grief you carry as a result. I again encourage you
to write about them in your notebook. More important, find
a safe person with whom you can share your grief. Such grief
is not meant to be carried alone. It is a weight meant to be
shared. Another's participation will not remove the grief, but
in some mysterious way, a loving and safe companion as you

walk through this valley will make the load you carry a bit more bearable until the light begins to dawn.

To grieve is to pass through the valley of the shadow of death. Again, you cannot do such a thing alone. You will need someone to accompany you, someone to carry hope for you. Experiencing the grief often means finding yourself falling back on old self-destructive coping mechanisms. The new ones don't seem strong enough to bear the weight of the grief. It can be a discouraging time. Death may feel like the only logical response. You will need another voice reminding you that yes, the losses are real, and yes, they are massive, but even as someone may attempt to bear those griefs with you, remember that there is Another who has truly born them. The prophet Isaiah said about Christ, "Surely he . . . carried our sorrows" (Isa. 53:4). There is a Redeemer who has come "to comfort all who mourn, and to provide for those who grieve" (Isa. 61:2-3).

Emotions are a part of our complexity as human beings. Emotions are given to us by God. They can change suddenly, and seemingly without cause. If we had no emotions, we would never feel joy, we would never laugh, and we would never feel love. However, having emotions also means having the capacity for fear, guilt, anger, and grief. We would like to hold on to the pleasant emotions but somehow get rid of the painful ones. A funny thing about emotions, though, is that if you deaden yourself to one side, the other goes with it. If you want to feel joy, you will have to deal with grief. If you want to feel love, you will have to face fear. As you begin to feel and struggle with emotions long dead, hold on tightly to the fact that as surely as you pass through the painful ones, so you will eventually come out on the other side. I clearly remember the day a survivor came into my office and with wonder in her voice said, "Something happened the other day, and I felt something I had never felt before. It took me a while until I realized that it was joy. I have never felt joy before, and it was wonderful!"

(If you need to read more about healing for your emotions before you go on to read the chapter about how abuse damaged your thinking, read chapter 19 next.)

15

Abuse Damaged
Your Thinking

No matter what your story is, regardless of the specific circumstances, if you have been sexually abused, your thinking has been damaged. It has either been shaped throughout childhood by lies and deceit, or it has been turned upside down by a sudden intrusion of violence. In either case, the work of discerning truth from lies is a big job. Let's listen to the voices of these survivors as they describe their distorted thinking, and then let's explore four areas affected by abuse: doublethink, dissociation, memory, and lies.

> *"My mind would ruminate on thoughts that would be against me as a person, against my worth, repeating old lies from my youth. My thoughts never rested. I would go from one negative, panicked thought to the next. I would draw conclusions about others and myself based*

*on thoughts and feelings that were not attached
to anything in the present."*

*"The eyes of an abused child see everything as
a blur. All truth is distorted."*

As we look now at the damage that was done to your thinking as
a result of the abuse, I would like you to keep a couple things in
mind. First, if the abuse occurred when you were small, remember that a child comes into this world knowing nothing and is
utterly dependent on adults to teach him or her about the self, the
world, God, and everything else. A child has no preexisting body
of knowledge with which to compare what is taught. Second, if
your abuse occurred somewhat later, remember that trauma shatters what we believed to be true about our world. Once you have
been raped, no matter how old you are, you don't just walk out
the door and assume you will be safe. You quit believing that if
you are good and responsible, things will turn out all right. The
ideas we all hold on to—that the world is a good, safe place or
that violence will never touch us—are destroyed.

DOUBLETHINK

In order to live with harsh realities, we sometimes do what
is called *doublethink:* we hold in our minds two contradictory
thoughts at the same time. Listen to the voice of this survivor
as on two different occasions she describes her father:

> *"My daddy was a wonderful man. Everybody
> loved him. My parents had parties and some-
> times let me come. He told jokes and entertained
> everybody. He provided a good living for 'his
> girls' (Mom and me and my two sisters)."*

> *"My father terrified me. He would drink and come
> after me and my sisters. We would hide in closets
> and under the bed. He always found one of us,
> and you could hear him raping whoever he caught.
> Mother was either gone or just cooking dinner.*
> They were such wonderful people. Why do
> you suppose they let that happen to us?"

If you grew up with a history of chronic sexual abuse and your
abuser was one of your caretakers, your mind had to do incred-
ible things so that you could survive. One aspect of that task
was to find a way to absolve your caretakers so you could continue to feel cared for or safe. As we said earlier, the most terrifying thought for small children who are abused is that they
are stuck for years with dangerous adults. It is an unbearable
thought. As a result, you may have developed doublethink.
For example, on the one hand you may have thought that your
mommy and daddy were dangerous and negligent people,
while at the same time you thought that they would take
good care of you. Another example of doublethink is thinking on the one hand that you have no hope of escape and on
the other hand that it will be better tomorrow. It is, literally,
double thinking. Somehow the mind splits so that both realities can be true. I have heard a survivor say: "Yes, my father
sexually abused me and was violent with me from the time
I was three until I left home—*but it is no big deal.* He didn't
mean it. He was a good provider." Logically, those two things
cannot be simultaneously true. Yet somehow, in the survivor's
mind, they are.

Another example is the young adult who was sexually
molested by someone he trusted: "My pastor sexually abused

me and threatened to destroy my family and my future if I told anyone—but I understand. He's a godly man, and I guess he was just struggling a little with his own weaknesses."

Are you aware of any ways that you use doublethink? One clue is when you think one thing and then your mind immediately responds with *Yes, but.* . . . For example, if I were to say to you, "Your father was an abuser," or "The rape was an awful thing," or "It must have been terrifying to go to your grandparents," and your first words are "Yes, but . . . ," then you have probably stumbled across a place where you doublethink. Write in your notebook any statements to which you would respond, "Yes, but. . . ."

DISSOCIATION

A mechanism not far removed from doublethink is *dissociation*. Many survivors simply refer to it as "spacing out." Dissociation helps a survivor get away physically or emotionally from the abuse. You can dissociate from the feelings in your body, from your emotions, or from the reality of what is happening. Some survivors do all three.

> *"He would turn me upside down on the bed and rape me. I would pick out a flower on the bedspread and concentrate on it. Eventually I would 'go into' the flower. Then I could not feel what he was doing."*

> *"I used to imagine a beautiful place full of flowers and a pretty lake. I would be a little girl running around and playing, sometimes flying a kite. I always went there when he raped me."*

The ability to dissociate is very high in school-age children. If you were that age when you were being abused, it is very likely that you used that capacity as a coping mechanism. But what was helpful to you as a child can be very dangerous to you as an adult. Being dissociated causes you not to notice all that is going on around you. That makes it much easier for you to get hurt. When you distance yourself from what is going on around you, then you tend to miss warning signs for danger.

Do you space out? If so, when does it happen? Do you know what triggers it? Write down your thoughts in your notebook.

MEMORY

The topic of memory is massive and cannot be adequately covered here. If you are interested in learning more about the relationship of sexual abuse and memory, read some of the books on the suggested reading list at the end of this book. For now, I simply want to make a few points that are important to know about yourself and also to know if you choose to get counseling.

Memory is a controversial topic today, and many people have very strong opinions about how memory works. It is also a relatively new field and therefore has not been intensively studied. New information is being acquired all the time. Let me suggest some guiding principles to help you as you process some of your own memories.

1. No set of symptoms automatically indicates a history of sexual abuse. Symptoms indicate damage. They do not always tell exactly what kind of damage has occurred. If someone tells you that your particular symptoms are proof that you were abused, whether or not you have any memory of being abused, that person has overstepped the bounds of good diagnosis and treatment.

2. *Memories can be repressed.* Children can do extraordinary things with their minds, as noted above, in order to hide the recollection of abuse. Vietnam veterans have done the same thing with the trauma they encountered. Many studies show how something long repressed can be suddenly remembered because an event triggered the recollection. One survivor said, "I kept the memory of my father's abuse out of my consciousness and very far away for many years. One day my adult son walked into the house, looking exactly like my father, and it all came crashing through my tidy walls."

3. *According to the research, traumatic events appear to be stored in the memory in vivid detail and create lasting visual images.* It has been suggested that memories of trauma are stored in a visual/behavioral memory system rather than the verbal memory system, which carries normal narrative autobiographical memory.

4. *Memories are not always accurate.* When an event occurs, the brain perceives it, stores it, and then recalls it. Things such as interpretation, mind-set, and attitudes can all affect recall. For example, you may recall a childhood home as being huge. Yet when you return as an adult, you find it seems very small. Obviously, the memory of the house was stored from a child's perspective.

5. *While memories are important, they are not* all *that is important.* Simply remembering does not bring healing, and it will not bring about change. Truth is more important than memories. To live your life based on lies taught by the remembered events is destructive. Replacing the lies with the truth and, by

God's grace, choosing new ways to respond to your life is what will bring freedom and change.

LIES AND TRUTH

One of the major tasks in healing the damaged thinking that results from sexual abuse is identifying the lies and replacing them with the truth. In earlier chapters we already identified some of the lies: "I am worthless." "I am responsible." "I deserved it." There are many, many more. Some of you believe that love or intimacy will always result in abuse, so you will never let anyone get close to you. "I built a wall that not even God can get through." Some of you believe that facing the truth about your life would hurt and destroy you rather than set you free. "I cannot look; the pain will be too great." Some of you believe that love is possible only if you do everything right. "I have never been loved for who I *am,* only for what I *do.* I learned to perform to be loved." Some of you believe the lie that if people learned about who you really are, they would walk away in disgust. "I worked frantically to earn the respect and admiration of anyone I met. I believed I could control my relationships and preclude the possibility of anyone's becoming displeased with me. Perhaps I thought that by stuffing people full of me, giving them what I thought they wanted up front, I could prevent them from knowing my true self."

The great sadness about all of this is that you end up living your life on the basis of lies. It takes tremendous energy to maintain the lie that the abuse didn't really happen or that it was no big deal. That energy never gets freed up for other purposes. The lie that you are trash means you either live in a way that fulfills that or work excessively to pretend to be otherwise so no one will figure it out. The lie that you have to perform to be loved means you can never stop. And on it goes. It is a sad and awful prison. You were not meant to live that way.

Try to identify some of the twisted thinking and the lies that you believe as the result of the abuse done to you. Take some time to write in your notebook some of the lies that you have come to believe about yourself, relationships, or God. What did your abuse teach you?

As we have said before, our God is a God of truth. Jesus said that he is the truth (John 14:6). The Holy Spirit is given to us in part to guide us into all truth (John 16:13). Jesus says that the truth sets us free (John 8:32). Ultimately, that means that knowing Christ himself is what gives us freedom. You will find, however, that as you seek after him who *is* truth, he will expose more and more of the lies and deception with which you live. Healing will not come through maintaining those lies. Although looking at the truth is one of the most terrifying things you may do, it *will* set you free. I know. I have watched it happen again and again.

(If you need to read more about healing for your thinking before you go on to read the chapter about how abuse damaged your relationships, read chapter 20 next.)

16

Abuse Damaged
Your Relationships

Sexual abuse occurs in the context of relationships. It is something that happens between two (or more) people. It is not hard to see, then, that abuse has a profound impact on how we think about and function in relationships. Sexual abuse affects our relationships in the areas of trust, boundaries, and control. Listen to the voices of these survivors:

> *"I related to others through the grid of abuse. I did not trust anyone very much. But I also did the opposite. I would trust people too much, depending on them to be like God. I did not have healthy boundaries or realistic expectations. I created an all-or-nothing standard for everyone: Either be like God, or I will have nothing to do with you."*

"I went to a pastor for advice and counseling. It was a vulnerable time in my life. I had certain feelings that something was not quite right, but I ignored the warning signals. Instead of listening to my own instincts, I decided to trust this man because of his position of authority. He was not trustworthy at all. I gave him control of my emotions and did not listen when my inner spirit was disturbed. He abused me sexually and other ways as well."

"I could relate only to people who would agree with me. If anyone disagreed, I would pull away. I knew nothing about compromise. I did not know how to have a mutual relationship. If my husband did not do things the way I wanted, I would retreat and become silent. I think it was simply a strategy to control people close to me."

"I knew nothing about privacy in relationships. People just walked into bathrooms and bedrooms unannounced. The concept of telling someone not to come in is very difficult for me. It feels as if I am doing something wrong. Saying no to someone is foreign to me."

"Trust is a really scary word. It strikes me as a very stupid thing to do. It was a given that my parents would hurt me. I never questioned that. In fact, all of the adults in my life either hurt me or ignored the fact that others did. I guess I

do trust then, don't I? I just trust that people
will hurt me or ignore me, that's all."

Living in relationship is a core part of who we are as humans.
God did not create us to live alone. He wants us to live in
relationship with himself and with each other. We all want
to know and be known, to love and be loved. We long to
speak or express ourselves in relationship with others. We
long to matter, to have impact, to be significant. Knowing,
loving, speaking, and mattering are marred for all of us
because of sin. Such things are damaged in crucial ways when
sexual abuse occurs.

Abuse destroys relationship. Instead of being known, we
are hidden. Instead of being loved, we are used. Instead of
having a voice, we are silenced. Instead of having an impact on
life and others, we do not matter. The lessons learned in such
an environment are powerful. They are also full of lies. These
lies are assumed to be truth. Relationships become painful,
frightening, chaotic places. We either relentlessly pursue relationships because of the longings we cannot still, although we
abhor ourselves for having them, or we fear and avoid relationships because of the danger they bring.

One survivor described her damaged relationship like this:
"My mother was selfish, anorexic, alcoholic, and self-absorbed.
She often humiliated me. One day I told her I would never
trust her again. She had humiliated me for the last time. I
called her a liar and told her she was a horrible mother. It cost
me a beating, but it didn't really hurt because of my decision
to hold her at arm's length. I never, ever let her near my heart
again."

Like all of the other areas damaged by sexual abuse, the area of relationships is massive. Volumes are written about relationships and how to conduct them. We will simply consider three areas that are damaged by sexual abuse.

Keep in mind as we discuss some of these things that you and I are learning all the time. We take what happens to us and process it, trying to make sense out of it and then acting on what we have learned. Children do not have the advantage of prior knowledge; they have no way of knowing whether or not what they are learning is true. However, while adults have the advantage of prior knowledge, that knowledge is helpful only if what was learned earlier is actually true. If the prior knowledge is a lie, then all incoming information will get filtered through that lie, and the lie will stand. This is especially so if the lie was repeated many times and accompanied by high emotional intensity.

TRUST

All of us trust. Some people trust that good will happen. Others of us trust that bad will happen. Perhaps some trust that some of both will happen. It is important for you to figure out what you have learned about trust in relationships and whether or not it is true. We act on what we trust to be true. I set my alarm at night because I trust that morning will come. I make dinner for my family because I trust that they will show up. I show up at work at certain times because I trust that my clients will meet me at their stated appointment times.

Some kinds of trust get a bit more risky and expose us to the potential of more hurt. If, for some reason, my family failed to show up for dinner, I could roll with it, especially if it was not something they typically do. However, I also trust

my husband to be faithful to me, my children to be honest
with me, and my friends not to gossip about or slander me.
Obviously, if any one of those things happened, I would
be deeply hurt, and my trust of those people would waver.
I would wonder if trusting them was a stupid idea.

We also come to trust in negative things. If every time
I walk around the block, a neighbor's dog chases me, I will
come to trust that the dog will come after me. If every time
I spoke to a particular person at church, that person stepped
on my foot, I would trust that to happen again and find a way
to protect my foot.

Again, such trust spills over into far more important
arenas. If my father, uncle, or brother abused me, I will probably not trust men. If my parents neglected me, I will not
trust that my needs will be met in relationships.

To trust in something means to rely on its integrity. If
something has integrity, it means it is the same all the way
through. To trust someone is to feel confident that the person
is who he or she appears to be. If you have shown yourself to
be faithful to me, if you say that you will be faithful to me,
then I trust that to be the truth. If you seem honest and if
you have integrity, then I will find you to be honest no matter
where or how I encounter you.

Remember the discussion about doublethink in the previous chapter? One of the most dangerous aspects of such thinking is that you learn to ignore parts of your reality. In order to
cope with the reality that your grandfather is unsafe, your
mind holds on to the belief that he is safe. Many survivors live
as if the unsafe is safe because acknowledging danger when
there is no escape is unbearable. The survivor who ignored the
warning signals suggesting that her pastor was not safe is an

illustration of where such thinking can lead. She learned through childhood sexual abuse to ignore warnings because they frightened her and because she could do nothing about them anyway. The result is that she learned to trust others to be one thing when all evidence indicated the opposite. She trusted her pastor to protect and lead her even though the warning signs suggested that he was a predator.

Abuse, then, can result in difficulties with trust. Some of you trust everyone because your longing for safe relationships is so great that you will try anyone and anything. Some of you trust no one. All relationships are seen through the grid of abuse. You believe that if you let others get too close, they will hurt you. You live behind a protective wall that is unscalable. Others of you trust even when the warning bells are going off in your head, and you end up in relationships that are abusive, telling yourself lies so you can believe they are good relationships.

Learning how to manage trust in realistic ways is often difficult for survivors. Whom can you trust? What are warning signs that someone is untrustworthy? What are realistic expectations for trusting a fallen human being? What can you trust them for? How can you learn to trust in healthy, truthful ways and not get set up to be abused again?

Try to figure out your patterns of trust or distrust in relationships. Do you trust anyone? How do you decide whether or not to trust someone? What do you do if a person fails to prove trustworthy? Are you trustworthy? What can others trust they will get from you? Does trusting frighten you, or do you do it blindly? Do you ever try to control others so you can guarantee a safe outcome for yourself in the relationship? Take some time to answer these questions in your notebook.

BOUNDARIES

Sexual abuse is a gross violation of boundaries. It is trespassing of the vilest sort. Something is taken from you, used, and tossed aside. How you feel and what you think or want are totally ignored.

> *"I have always done everything that was asked of me. I never told my husband no, my children no, or people at church no. I lived as if I had no limitations. Eventually, I couldn't do it anymore, and I simply broke down. Learning limits has been an arduous process for me."*

> *"My family trespassed all over each other. There were no lines, no privacy, no limits. I did a lot of socially inappropriate things for years and was very embarrassed to learn that they were things you 'just don't do.' I asked questions I should not have asked, took things from others without asking permission, opened doors and drawers without anyone's consent. For a long time I never wanted to go out anywhere because I felt as if I had no idea what the rules were. It was better just to hide. It feels pretty stupid to be an adult and have no idea what is proper."*

> *"One of the results of the abuse for me was that I focused on other people to the exclusion of myself. Now I realize I am a separate individual, not simply part of someone else. I was all wrapped up in 'fixing' other people so I would feel better. It never occurred to me to look at myself."*

*"The rapist took my money. He took my posses-
sions. He took my sense of safety in my home. He
took my body. I did not give permission. My
refusal was ignored. He walked all over my life
with no regard for me."*

When God created human beings, he gave us a voice, a means
of expressing ourselves out in the world. God *wants* us to
express ourselves. Scripture tells us about God's voice all the
way through. Jesus is called *the Word.* Sexual abuse silences the
victim's voice because any resistance or any refusal does not
matter. The victim's voice and words are disregarded.

One survivor put it this way: "My abuser did a master-
ful job of silencing me. When I said, 'No, I don't want to,' he
forced me to do it anyway. He hushed me when he was fondling me. Then he would push my face into the bed during
sex. Finally he would strangle me until I passed out. It was
often a very literal, physical silencing."

Boundaries are easily trounced when voice is silenced.
When survivors live in an environment in which the abuser
takes what he or she should ask for and refuses to give what
the victim requests, they feel violated. Survivors feel as if they
never know when the boom will fall. Either they respond by
assuming that they have no right of refusal and that others
have the right to take from them, or they become hypervigi-
lant about boundaries and patrol their own like a sentry on
duty, protecting and guarding themselves meticulously.

Some survivors struggle to see that they have any right to
say no or any right to draw a line. One client was stunned to
realize that saying no to her father (who was still abusing her
as an adult) was the right thing to do before God. She said,

"I thought I had to obey my father no matter what." When you are unable to draw lines, you become subject to any evil any human being may want to perpetrate against you. When your voice is silenced, you are unable to call evil by its right name, to say, "I can't let you do that to me because it is against God."

Many survivors believe they have to answer any question anyone asks them. The concept of saying, "I would rather not answer that" does not feel like an option. If you are like this, you believe that you have to give whatever anyone wants from you. It doesn't matter if you can't give it or if you don't want to give it or if you believe it is wrong to give it. You feel that you have no voice and no choice.

Other survivors have difficulty setting limits. One survivor had just delivered a new baby, but when her husband asked her to have sex, she felt she had to say yes. Some days you may be exhausted and overcommitted, but if someone asks you a favor, you feel as if you must say yes. It doesn't occur to you to say, "I am tired; I need to stop" or "I can't do that right now" or "I am sick and need to go to bed." You live your life not as a finite human being but as a person with no boundaries, no limits. In other words, your life is based on a lie. It is easy then to become sleep deprived, to be overwhelmed, and eventually to break down.

The flip side is to spend life patrolling your boundaries, fearful that someone will take what you don't want to give. Certainly others have done so. What you do give is meted out carefully, and when you are asked to give again, you feel panic. One survivor described it this way: "I see now that many of my choices have been based on fear. All my relationships were governed by fear. Whenever anyone asked me for time or love or commitment, I panicked. I think I believed that if I let down my guard at all and gave anything, they would come in and take it all. I watched what I gave like a hawk and never, until recently, knew what it was like to give freely and graciously."

CONTROL

Sexual abuse often leads to a very high need to control relationships. Fear runs very deep too. All of these difficult struggles affect intimacy in relationships in complex ways. The longing for intimacy pushes us toward others. The fear of abuse, rejection, pain, and damage holds us back. We need and want relationship. However, abuse teaches that safety does not come in relationships with people because people bring pain. It is a staggering dilemma that reverberates through the lives of survivors.

Give thought to some of your relationship patterns. How do you try to control others? Do you feel able to maintain healthy boundaries? Do you exercise your voice effectively in relationship? Write your responses and insights in your notebook.

Is there hope for healthy relationships? Yes. You do not need to be stuck. The prophet Isaiah says the following in speaking about redeemed Israel: "It will no longer be said to you, 'Forsaken,' nor to your land will it any longer be said, 'Desolate.' . . . [You will be called] 'the holy people, the redeemed of the Lord' " (Isa. 62:4, 12, NASB). I have prayed that those words would become a reality for many survivors, and I have seen those prayers answered. May it be so for you as well.

(If you need to read more about healing for your relationships before you go on to read the chapter about how abuse damaged you spiritually, read chapter 21 next.)

17

Abuse Damaged
Your Spirit

Sexual abuse touches the spiritual area deeply. It shakes to
the core our beliefs about God and how he perceives and
treats us. It hinders our ability to hope. Listen to these
survivors' voices:

> "As a child I was betrayed, abandoned, and
> sexually abused. I concluded that God was
> untrustworthy, that he had also abandoned me,
> and that he also was unsafe and abusive. How
> was I to know anything different? It all made
> sense. It fit together."

> "The impact of my abuse on my relationship
> with God has taken awhile for me to see. I
> became a Christian as a teen. I believed God
> loved me, but I notice now that my journaling
> showed times when I was actually fearful of

God. I was afraid he, too, would abuse and hurt me. As I began to heal, my view of God did too. I am learning to trust him for who he really is, a loving and forbearing God."

"I began to believe that my very creation was an accident of God's. If God was all-knowing and all-loving, how could he have allowed me into this awful family, devoid of love and full of self-pity, hate, and chaos? How could he have put me, someone who longed to love and be loved, into all this abuse and neglect? I would never settle with him hating me. Instead, I believed that God had somehow missed me, not noticed my creation. I was unintentionally created. Incorrectly made. This dark assumption accompanied me into my adult life and fashioned my thinking."

"I have lived terrified of God, certain that if I crossed him in any way, I would get beaten."

"The abused child's eyes see God as a very big judge. I believed that if he saw what I was doing, then my punishment would be eternal. Surely he could never love me or care for me."

RECONCILING GOD AND EVIL

Survivors struggle to understand how to put together an understanding of God with the abuse they suffered at the hands of another human being. Elie Wiesel, one of the foremost writers on the Holocaust, says that we are wrong to assume that it is a consolation to believe that God is alive. Rather than being the solution, saying that God is alive simply states the problem. He talks about his struggle with two apparently irreconcilable realities—the reality of God and the reality of Auschwitz. Each seems to cancel out the other, but neither will disappear. Either alone could be managed—Auschwitz and no God, or God and no Auschwitz. But how does one handle Auschwitz *and* God?

Many of you will identify with Wiesel's struggle. You can make sense of sexual abuse and no God, or God and no sexual abuse. But how do you tolerate the two realities together? Many of you have concluded that God is unloving or at least does not love you. You feel that he, too, has discarded you as unworthy, insignificant.

The following expression, voiced by a young girl, captures not only her thinking on the matter but possibly yours as well: "Sex is really bad because it hurts really bad and sometimes I bleed and that's yucky. When Daddy does sex to me I feel sad. But I gotta act happy so nobody [k]nows I was bad. I think sex should be agenst the law because it hurts. My Mister Jesus he just watched and he didn't make it stop. But _____ sez that Mister Jesus writed it down in a big book and my daddy's got lots of xplaning to do when he sees Mister Jesus. But I'm still mad at Mister Jesus cuz that sex hurted and it was bad and he didn't stop it."

Please stop and let yourself speak about what you just read. What are you thinking? What are you feeling? How does this affect where you are with God? Again, remember, we are looking for truth. Do not be afraid to speak it out loud or write it in your notebook. Change and healing cannot come to what lies unexposed.

"I THOUGHT AS A CHILD"

Two important factors affect the thinking of someone who has been abused as a child: how children learn and how trauma affects them. These two factors influence how you think about and relate to God.

How Children Learn

Children learn about the unseen by way of the seen; they learn about the invisible by way of the visible. They think concretely, not abstractly. Children understand the love of God by seeing how their parents love each other or love them. Children grasp the concept of faithfulness when they have adults who respond faithfully to them. They learn about truth when parents live and speak truth before them, even when it would be easier not to.

Adults, who can think abstractly, also learn this way. That is why Jesus used illustrations involving common elements to explain the things of God. He used water, bread, vines, and light to communicate the mysteries of heaven to us. When what we learn in the visible world gives us incorrect information about the invisible world, we get very confused.

Think about the little girl whose daddy prayed with her and then abused her, saying that God told daddies to love their little girls that way. Think about the young boy whose counselor at a Christian camp represents authority and what is good, but who then lures him aside to molest him. Think about the young girl whose pastor, a representative of God, encourages her to share confidences with him and then rapes her.

Each of these people was taught that God is love, a refuge, truth, and holiness—but what they experienced at the hands of the people who taught them these things was pain, betrayal, lies, and evil. What confusion! The lessons in the seen suggest the very opposite of the words spoken about God. Which are they to believe? The words say one thing, but their experience teaches another. No wonder Jesus said, "Whoever causes one of these little ones who believe in Me to stumble, it is better for him that a heavy millstone be hung around his neck, and that he be drowned in the depth of the sea. Woe to the world because of its stumbling blocks! For it is inevitable that stumbling blocks come; but woe to that man through whom that stumbling block comes!" (Matt. 18:6-7, NASB). Jesus knew the damage and confusion caused by anyone whose life serves as a stumbling block to others as they seek to understand God.

How Trauma Affects Children

The second factor affecting children's ability to understand and experience the truth of who God is lies in the nature of trauma itself. Trauma stops growth. It paralyzes. In order to survive, the person needs to push aside the trauma in some fashion. Life goes on, and so does much growth, but the trauma itself and the lessons derived from that trauma are sealed away, unaffected by new experience and information. I often tell survivors that it is as if part of their thinking got frozen in time.

It is this aspect of "frozenness" that leads a muscular man, well over six feet tall, to feel very small in the presence of someone who reminds him of his abuser. When our thinking is frozen, we may encounter people who show themselves trustworthy, but somehow that experience does not touch the fear of trust brought about by the abuse. We continue to live as if no one has ever been trustworthy. It also means we hear and even believe many truths about God, but they don't seem to penetrate us. As one woman said, "I know Jesus loves me. I believe it to be true, but I have never *felt* that love. For some reason it won't go in." Essentially what happened to her has been sealed off behind a wall, and the place where she feels most unlovable cannot be touched.

HOPE

Sexual abuse also damages our ability to hope. Researchers have talked about what they call a "disorder of hope." Hope is the confidence that what we desire is truly possible. To be repeatedly abused and to be helpless to stop it is to experience the death of hope. Hope, then, becomes something to be feared and avoided; to hope is simply to set yourself up for being crushed again. Listen to the voices of these survivors:

> *"Once, I even told on one of my abusers. We ended up in court. The judge knew my family, and he threw out the case, sent me back to my stepfather's house, and forced me to publicly apologize to my abuser for being a liar. My abuser hugged me and kissed me in front of everyone, and he whispered in my ear that he would eventually get me for telling. I was alone. There was no hope."*

> *"One day I was working in the kitchen with my mommy. I was seven. I tried to tell her that Daddy was hurting me. She yelled at me for thinking bad thoughts about Daddy and said she did not want to hear another word out of me. It destroyed me. There was no longer any*

*reason to hope. If Mommy wouldn't help, then
who would?"*

Such lessons suggest that hope in God is at best foolish and
at worst dangerous. To live without hope is to live in a very
dark place.

So, sexual abuse throws the character of God into question, erodes trust, kills hope, and makes it seem impossible to
know the love and security of God. Some of you have coped
with this by keeping your abuse at bay, thinking it wasn't so
bad or important. That has enabled you to continue to hold
on to some of the truths about God you desperately want
and need to be true. You acknowledge the abuse in a cursory
fashion or not at all. It is Wiesel's option of "no Auschwitz
and God." Others of you know and face the truth of your
abuse, but God is absent, cruel, impotent, or capricious. You
have concluded that either you were not worth protecting,
God hates you, or he is ineffective. You live with the option
"Auschwitz and no God."

I believe God can stand up in the light of the abuse that
was done to you. You do not have to downplay it or pretty it
up in some fashion in order for him to exist and love you. I
certainly do not have all the answers. The problem of suffering
has remained mysterious in many minds far better than mine.
I do know, however, that there is a place that can include both
Auschwitz and God without altering the character of either
one. As we move on to the subject of healing in the various
arenas we have discussed, it is my hope and prayer that you
will begin to see the truth of this statement.

Part Four
What Does Healing Look Like?

THOSE of you who have read the previous section all the way through are probably feeling overwhelmed and perhaps a bit hopeless. It could have the same effect as looking around at a home that has been trashed and having no idea where to begin to restore order. The best solution may seem to be simply to sit down and cry. Actually, if that is how you feel, crying is probably a good idea.

I expect some of you think that everything I have said and more is true about you. What I have mentioned is by no means comprehensive. You may be able to see damage that wasn't discussed. Others of you may think I got a bit excessive because you relate to only a few parts. Wherever you are on that continuum, if you have been abused, you have been touched by evil. Evil has impact, as does good. You have been affected in some way. Some of you have been affected far more profoundly than others. There are many, many factors that contribute to the effect of sexual abuse. No two of you are alike.

Two things are important for you to know. First, you need to understand what the impact of the abuse has been. What has it taught you? How has it changed you? Where does it hurt you? Healing is applied knowledgeably only when the wound is understood. If you go to a doctor and simply say "I hurt" without giving any clue as to how or where, the doctor may give you an antibiotic when you need to have your bone set. The doctor needs to understand the injury before he or she can attempt to help. Similarly, the more you understand about the abuse that was done to you, the more you will know what kind of healing you need and where to find it.

Second, even if every aspect of damage I listed is true about you and you can add fifty more areas to that list, there is hope. No matter how badly you are wounded, there is hope for healing. Will you heal perfectly? No. Healing is a process, and growth is a lifetime thing. However, I know people who have experienced every aspect of damage we have considered and then some, and they are currently out there living, growing, relating, experiencing joy, and contributing.

How has such a thing happened? It has happened because there is a Redeemer. I know him, and I have seen his work. It is a good work, and he is faithful to it. You have heard me mention him often thus far. I hope that as we walk through the following chapters, you will meet him in new ways. I think he may surprise you. I hope so.

18

Healing for Your Body

In chapter 13 we considered how sexual abuse damaged your body. Let me remind you that there is hope. Healing *will* come for your body. It will come through reconnecting with your body and learning to think about it differently. Healing will come through the power of the Redeemer. Listen to the voices of these survivors:

> *"I am beginning to learn about the wholeness of self—body/mind/soul/spirit. My body is important. What I do to it and with it matters. But I am not just a body. I am finding I can have integrity all through. What happens in my body can actually be a truthful expression of my person. It never was before."*

> *"I worked hard all my life not to feel any physical sensations. It is grueling work to undo that. However, I just experienced something good with*

my body! I realized I could feel the softness of my children's skin. I had no idea it was so soft. It was the first time in many years I have felt anything. It is also the first time any touch has been good."

"I am learning to enjoy sex with my husband for the first time. I used to just wait for it to be over. I was very passive. I had no idea bodies could be enjoyable. Mine was simply one of the ways others hurt me."

THE JOURNEY TOWARD HEALING

The work of learning how to live differently in your body after it has been sexually abused is very hard work. It often takes a long time. If the abuse was chronic or if you also grew up battered, then it will be even more difficult. You will need help in this work, and you will probably need help from a counselor who understands how painstaking the task is. Someone will not simply be able to say, "Stop this," or "Start that," and have it suddenly be different. You will need someone to encourage you on your journey.

The first step requires that to some degree you get reconnected to your body. You can't respond appropriately to a body if you don't feel anything. I have worked with survivors who were deprived of food so much that they taught themselves not to feel hunger. If that physical signal doesn't get reconnected, how will they know when to eat? It will require time and energy to learn how to hear and respond to your body's signals.

If you have abused substances in order not to feel, you will have to get yourself into some kind of program to help you to stop using. If you are high all the time, you can't register pain or fear or anything else. You can't reconnect while anesthetized.

When my client survivors are really disconnected from their bodies, I begin with very simple assignments. I might suggest that they sit outside with their face pointed toward the sun and ask themselves questions like these: What does it feel like? Describe it. What do you like about it? What don't you like about it? Or I suggest that they wade in a creek or walk in the rain or tromp through the mud. I do make sure that at least as far as they know, nothing about my suggestion triggers a memory. The purpose of this assignment is to help with connection. If I tell someone to walk in the mud when he or she had been abused in the mud, then the assignment will foster disconnection!

If you need to reconnect with your body, try an activity similar to the ones I have just suggested. Then record your responses in your notebook.

What happens as you begin to feel what has been ignored? Fear kicks in very quickly! To feel anything will throw you right back into fear of the abuse. As soon as that happens, the old and faithful coping mechanisms will claw their way to the front. You may work yourself into a frenzy, exercise madly, binge and purge, drink, smoke pot, or hurt yourself. You may do anything not to feel. You may feel as if it's hopeless and want to give up. Don't.

Try this. Identify a response that you can use instead of the old response mechanism. For example, if your normal response is to binge, decide that you will go for a walk instead. If your old response is to turn to alcohol, decide that you will journal what you are feeling instead. If your typical response is to cut yourself, decide to call a friend instead. Redirect yourself, if only for five minutes. It will be a victory because you will have broken an old cycle for the first time. As you keep challenging the old behavior, little by little, you will eventually find that enough time has passed and you don't "need" that behavior anymore. It is an awesome moment!

A great many coping mechanisms are destructive. The cycle is very similar to the abuse cycle. You feel; it hurts; you find some way to disconnect. Very often that disconnection is brought about by something that is self-destructive to you. You feel; it hurts; you cut. You feel; it hurts; you drink. You feel; it hurts; you work yourself into the ground. What you needed when the abuse occurred was safety, comfort. When the fear sets in, that is *still* what you need. This exercise is intended to help you find ways to provide safety and comfort for yourself by what you do or by the people you seek out.

You will discover over time that you have the power to choose what to do with your body. That means you can choose not to have it abused. Not only that, you can choose what will be done with it and find that it can be used (*your* body!) to glorify God.

Listen to the words of a survivor as she has wrestled with the impact of abuse on her body: "In wrestling with the effects of abuse on my body, I have found it helpful to think of my body as a house. Jesus is the carpenter. He created me and gave me to my parents, who were to be the initial 'caretakers' of this house. They took my house and destroyed it. They smashed holes in the walls. They left the windows open, and rain rotted the structure.

"After a time the house was given to me. It was in total disrepair. No one cared for it. No one wanted to be around it. No one loved it. Some people came and tried to care for it, but they walked away. It was hopeless. I did not want to work on my house either. I hated it. I scratched at it. I banged it up. I tore at it. I knew no other way to care for it.

"In the midst of my despair, I had a visit from the carpenter. He offered himself to me. He would take up residence in my home and help me rebuild. At first I didn't want to let him in. How could he live in such a mess? The house was terrible. Besides, why had he waited until now to come? Would he really love this house or simply say it needed to be demolished?

"Eventually I asked him to come. Together we started to rebuild my house. I wanted the outside fixed first. He started on the inside. Little by little he takes out the damage and repairs it. With gentleness he sands and refines his work. He engages me in the process. He patiently teaches me how to do the work.

"This house is my body. I find that as the carpenter teaches me that my body is precious and worthy of protection, I am gradually learning to treat it with appreciation rather than disgust. The impulses to attack my body on the outside are diminishing. It is a long, hard battle, but the carpenter is faithful."

THE VOICE OF THE REDEEMER

In chapter 13 we spoke about the fact that Jesus, who is the Redeemer, inhabited a body like ours. I would like you to consider two things based on that truth. First, what was it like for Jesus, who was himself God, to live in a body? Was his experience at all similar to yours? Second, what does this Jesus say to you about living in your body? Does the fact that he lived in one have anything to do with how you live in yours?

Scripture tells us that God is all-powerful, all-sufficient, and all-knowing. He is sovereign over all. He created and sustains all life. Yet somehow, he who is all-powerful became weak. He who is all-sufficient became dependent. He who is all-knowing became finite. He became a baby. We have talked in previous chapters about what it means to be a baby. Babies can't do very much. They know almost nothing, and they are utterly dependent on others to take care of them. He who created life had to be fed. He who knew all had to be taught. He who sustained all had to be carried. Where you lived, he has lived. He *knows* what it is like to be little. He *knows* what it is like to be helpless and at the mercy of others.

More astounding than that is the fact that he was subject to these things not only as a child but also as an adult. Listen to some of what is recorded in the Old Testament prophecy of Isaiah. He grew like "a root out of dry ground" (Isa. 53:2). Some of you are like that. The fact that you grew at all is amazing. By rights you should be dead or crazy. All you had around you was dry ground. Nothing grows in dry ground. Barren places yield no fruit. Yet somehow, from a barren place, you have grown in some measure. Thirsty, yes. Alone, yes. So was he.

Isaiah goes on to describe Jesus. "He had no beauty or majesty to attract us to him, nothing in his appearance that we should desire him" (Isa. 53:2). Some of you hate your bodies. You find nothing good or attractive about them. You wonder what it is like to feel attractive to someone. He who created all beauty was not beautiful. He who was king over all failed to appear majestic. He *knows* what it is like not to be desired.

He was "stricken . . . smitten . . . and afflicted" (Isa. 53:4). Many of you have been hit, injured, wounded, and scarred. Some of you can point to scars on your body or scars on your soul as a result of the abuse. You know the searing pain, the bleeding, the humiliation of being made a mess and then discarded. You look at your scars and want them eradicated because they are proof of your humiliation. They remind you of the pain. He who healed everything imaginable—the blind, the deaf, the crippled, the demonized—is scarred. The Healer felt pain beyond words. He *knows*.

In the New Testament account of Jesus' death, we are told, "When the soldiers crucified Jesus, they took his clothes" (John 19:23). To have someone take your clothes against your will is a shaming, humiliating thing. You are exposed. You want to hide or die. Many of you have had your clothes taken by evil men and women. Evil men took Jesus' clothes and raised him up, exposed for all to see. Jesus knows how hurtful and humiliating it feels not to have clothes on. He *knows*.

In his suffering and death Jesus chose to experience abuse, rejection, pain, wounding. He *chose* to enter into your experience, one about which you had no choice. He allowed himself to be treated as if he were helpless to restrain it or stop it. He chose to be spit on, struck, exposed, tortured, restrained, and used. Has that not been the experience many of you have had? When you cry out to Jesus, he *knows*. When the pain is so great it makes you scream, he *knows*. He cried out. He screamed. He entered into your suffering and abuse so that when you come to him with a broken body, an abused body, a humiliated body, you will know with certainty that you speak to one who *knows*.

I urge you to allow yourself the space and time to meditate on these things. Go to the Scriptures for yourself. Ask God to help you hear and see the truth about Jesus, God who lived in a body. Think about why he did that. Why did he subject himself to such limitation and humiliation? Think about what that means. Consider the cross simply from a "body" stand-point. What happened there? What was it like? Do such truths have anything to say to you as you struggle with your own abuse, your own life in a body? Write down your insights in your notebook. Share them with a trusted friend or counselor.

Remember the three truths we spoke about in chapter 13? We said that your body was created by God himself, that he chose to inhabit a body, and that he is willing to do so again because he wants to dwell in yours. If you know Christ as the Savior, he does dwell in your body. We also said that *no amount* of abuse nullifies those truths. No matter how violently, sadis-tically, perversely you were abused, if you know the Redeemer, he dwells in *your* body. What does that mean?

Our body is the medium through which we live. Everything we do, say, feel, or think is through the body. We cannot live or express ourselves without it. The Bible does not see our body as a hindrance, a clog, an annoyance, or some-thing that gets in our way. Instead, Scripture says our body is "a temple of the Holy Spirit" (1 Cor. 6:19, NASB). Our body is not to be despised. It has great value.

The apostle Paul says, "I urge you . . . to offer your bodies as living sacrifices . . . to God" (Rom. 12:1). Ask yourself these questions: Whose character or personality is manifested through my body? Who is exhibited through my hands, my eyes, my mouth, my thinking, and my loving? You express your character through the body. You cannot express a character without a body. We spoke about how abusers are expressing their character through their body. What abusers do is a manifestation of who *they* are, not who *you* are. Conversely, what you do is a manifestation of who you are. What character is manifested through your body? Did you learn the lessons so well that you manifest the character of your abuser in the way you treat your body? Or has fear held you so tightly that you manifest the character of a victim long after the victimizing has stopped?

Your body is to be the temple of the Holy Spirit. That means your body is the medium for expressing the character of Jesus. That wonderful character, expressed through a body two thousand years ago, would like to be expressed through yours. Scripture does not see our bodies as things to be disregarded or ignored. God elevated the human body by choosing to be present in one. He wants to be present in yours as well.

By implication, then, we need to care for our body, protecting it from evil and maintaining its integrity. This is not hopeless or impossible just because abuse has occurred. Working such truths out in your body may be a more difficult task for you because of your abuse. They are, however, *truths for you*. Our great Redeemer can do the work necessary in you so that your body might serve as his temple in word and in deed. It is a marvelous thing to see a body that has been used, sold, mutilated, and scarred become a body redeemed for the Master's use—holy and undefiled. "Christ *in* you, the hope of glory" (Col. 1:27, emphasis added). How I long for each of you to understand these truths so that you will be able to live with the beauty of our God on and in you!

19

Healing for Your Emotions

I n chapter 14 we considered how sexual abuse damaged
your emotions. Let me remind you that there is hope.
Healing *will* come for your emotions. It will come
through giving voice to your emotions. Healing will come
through the power of the Redeemer. Listen to the voices of
these survivors:

> *"I thought my grief would swallow me whole.*
> *It was so great I couldn't see or feel anything*
> *else. I shut down. I am on the other side now. I*
> *thought that was impossible. Does the grief still*
> *hit? Sure, but I have also felt delight, joy, and*
> *even peace. I used to think I was incapable of*
> *such feelings."*
>
> *"I have hope. I fought it for a long time. I think*
> *it was there before I would admit it. It is a*

*different kind of hope than I felt as a kid. Then
I just hoped things would turn out okay. Do
I still want that? Of course. But I have a
greater hope now. I have the certain hope that no
matter what, Christ can redeem whatever happens. I have seen life come out of the death in my
life.* I know *it can happen."*

THE JOURNEY TOWARD HEALING

As we continue to consider what healing looks like, I want
to remind you of the fact that in many ways we are making arti-
ficial divisions. It is not hard to see how complex we as humans
are and how one area runs into another. In Psalm 139 David
talks about our being knit together. That means all the parts
of us are entwined together. To pull on one thread is to touch
all the others. In reality, the threads of our being are woven
together in such complexity that we cannot really just take out
one piece and look at it without considering the whole.

The truth of our wholeness, our entwining, is part of the
reason that sexual abuse has such an impact on people. Our
sexuality is a core part of who we are. You cannot be a person
and not be a gender. They are both present at birth. They
are inseparable to some degree. To abuse people sexually is
to attack their person, not just their body. You cannot have a
person without a body. It is also true that because we are knit
together, you cannot damage the body without impact on the
mind, the emotions, and every other aspect of who we are.
To think that might be possible is to deny how we are made.
That is why when people say to me, "I was sexually abused for
five years, but it is no big deal," I know that is not truth. Such
a statement denies who God says we are.

Having said all that, we will proceed to look at who we are in parts anyway! It is easier and a bit more manageable that way. Just keep in mind that there is a certain artificiality to it.

Giving Voice to Your Emotions

We talked in chapter 14 about how fear is the core response to trauma. To be traumatized is to be helpless. To be helpless in the face of an atrocity is to feel terror. We lose our sense of control, and we disconnect. The trauma of sexual abuse occurs in the context of relationship (unlike, for example, trauma due to a natural disaster). Recovery—learning not to live based on the fear—must also occur in the context of relationship. It cannot occur in isolation. Fear destroys trust. Fear inhibits love. Fear results in constriction, restraint, retreat. All of these profoundly affect our relationships.

The need to experience a healing, safe relationship often leads survivors to consider counseling. To be in a relationship with a safe person who also understands sexual abuse and its consequences can result in phenomenal healing. It is also this need for relationship that makes the support network of a loving church community (one that is also educated about sexual abuse) an immeasurable gift. My experience is that survivors who are blessed with both of these resources recover more quickly and more fully. If you are stuck somewhere without either of these options, is healing still possible? Yes. God has the wonderful capacity of not being limited by such things. However, generally he works through relationships like these.

Let me suggest some things you might do to help process some of your fear. First (dare I say it again?), you need to articulate the fear. Trauma shuts us up. You need to put words to your fear. Sometimes survivors resist when I keep telling them to write or to journal. "I can't. I never have. I have nothing to say." Little by little they find words. One woman wrote down some things for me. She had never written anything before except as it was required by school. She was astonished that she could write and equally astounded at how it helped.

Some of you will get stuck. You will not be able to find words. Try making a collage that expresses how you feel. Use the words of other survivors, perhaps some that you have read in this book. Say them out loud. Change them as it occurs to you to do so. Paint, draw, sculpt with clay. One survivor could not seem to get over the obstacle of articulating the first memory she wanted to speak to me about. She was a dancer. I sent her home to create a dance that expressed what happened and what she felt about it. She did, and it jarred the words loose. Some survivors have brought me music they have composed or heard. We have used that to help me explore with them words that could possibly express their experience. Use colors. What colors accurately represent how you feel?

Why is finding words for your fear so important? Maybe I just have a thing about words. But I don't think that's all. We discussed in chapter 16 that God created us with a voice and that he intends for us to use it. However, that voice is lost when fear overwhelms. Perhaps you have seen others who were afraid. Either they are rendered speechless, or at best, they stutter inarticulately. Your voice is part of the image of God in you. It is intended to be a powerful force within you. Voice matters. *Your* voice matters.

Another reason why finding words is so important is that when we are overwhelmed by fear and shut up, then we get

stuck. The brain, which is constantly processing things, has
no opportunity to process what happened. The fear just sits in
there, untouched. Not only that, it keeps showing up. What
happened keeps intruding. The past becomes the present
again and again. That happens in many ways. Flashbacks are
one way that fear manifests itself. Or perhaps jumping every
time someone comes into a room. You jump not because *that*
person has ever hurt you but because a long time ago someone
did. Your mind will not separate the past and the present adequately unless it is allowed to process, to articulate, to express
what happened, and to find a way to live with it.

The final and very important reason to learn to give voice
to your experience and your response to it, is so you can learn
to separate the truth from the lies. This is crucial for dealing with fear and guilt and anger and grief. When you were
abused, you were helpless. Somewhere along the way came the
moment of terror when you realized you couldn't stop what
was happening. There was nothing you could do to make it
not happen. When you were abused, you were overwhelmed.
The fear, the panic, the pain, the questions were too much.
So you shut down, unhooked, went away. When you were
abused, you may have felt anger. Maybe you felt it later. You
were angry at the evil, the injustice, the pain. When you
were abused, you longed for safety, for comfort. You wanted
someone to come and care for you, hold you, tell you it would
never happen again. Safety became paramount.

In the context of abuse, all of those things are true. You
couldn't stop it. It was overwhelming. Anger is appropriate.
And you did indeed need safety and comfort. However, when
abuse is not dealt with properly, those truths inevitably lead
to life-destroying lies. "Nothing I do in life matters." "I can't

handle anything." "If you cross me, I will rage." "I deserve my rage for letting the abuse happen." "I am stupid to want what I can't have—safety, comfort." "Nobody in all the world will ever extend comfort to me; I just have to take care of myself." "I don't need anybody." "I need comfort so badly that I will take anything I get."

Do you hear the lies? Or maybe you don't. Maybe you hear those statements as true and think I am finally getting it! No such luck! I will continue to encourage you to give voice to your experience, to tell the truth—preferably in a safe relationship—so you can begin to allow God to help sort out truth from lies.

Each of these emotions—fear, guilt, anger, and grief—warrants a chapter or more in itself. Not only do the lies need to be separated from the truth, but dealing with these feelings and their effects on you will require hard work and a lot of repetition. Don't be discouraged by the repetition. It's normal to need it. A statement like "Oh, you shouldn't feel guilty about that" will not result in your guilt disappearing! You will need to understand your guilt, separate lies from truth, hear truth over and over again, study what God says, and then turn around and do it all over again. The task is difficult. It is not impossible. Its difficulty is, I believe, part of why Jesus said how terrible it is to cause a little one to stumble. Healing is possible, in spite of that, because God longs for you to live in the freedom that truth provides and will patiently repeat what you need to hear from him as long as it takes.

THE VOICE OF THE REDEEMER

When we talked about the body, we said that Jesus inhabited a body like ours. Well, not only did he have a body like ours, he also felt emotions like ours. Somewhere we have gotten the idea that Christians are not supposed to have or exhibit too many feelings. This is certainly more true about what we would call negative feelings. However, even too much of the good feelings makes a lot of people squirm. We seem to label people who weather any crisis with little or no emotion as "spiritually mature" people. If that is true, then Jesus was not very spiritual on some occasions. Let's take a look.

Did Jesus ever feel fear? Consider the Garden of Gethsemane, where Jesus spent the night before he was crucified. Jesus was in anguish, in agony. He begged the Father to let the cup pass from him. What is that about? The cup that Jesus speaks of is the cup of God's wrath. *All* of the wrath of God poured out on all of the sin of the world. Jesus was going to experience the unadulterated anger of the Father while being abandoned by the Father. That is the most frightening place that exists. Jesus did not want to go. He did not approach the cross serenely. Many martyrs have gone to their deaths serenely. Jesus did not.

Some of you have felt anguish, agony. You have felt terror at what lies ahead. Jesus knows what that feels like. Some of you have begged someone to stop, and they did not. Jesus knows what that's like. Some of you know the experience of feeling a human being's wrath poured out on you. He *knows*. Jesus did not go to his execution with joy. He went with agony. He endured the cross for the sake of the joy it would lead to. Crosses are not places of joy but of pain and terror and abandonment. Abuse is not a place of joy. It, too, is a place of pain and terror and abandonment. He *knows*.

What about guilt? Surely the Son of God never felt guilt. After all, he was sinless. What did he have to feel guilty about? It is true that he was without sin. He never did, said, thought, or felt anything wrong. We are told, however, that he who was without sin *became* sin (2 Cor. 5:21). If he became sin, what did that make him? It made him guilty. Isaiah says his life was a guilt offering (Isa. 53:10). The guiltless was made guilty.

Notice two important truths here. First, some of you know what it is to be treated as guilty when in fact you are guiltless. Jesus has been there too. Unlike Jesus, you are not guilty for what someone else did to you. You may have *felt* like a guilt offering, but you will not be held guilty. Second, Jesus was made to be a guilt offering so that you could be clean—free of guilt. So where you are not guilty, he knows. And where you are guilty, he has offered himself so you might be free.

What about anger? Did Jesus get angry? We are told of several occasions when Jesus got angry. He was angry with the Pharisees because they did not want him to heal on the Sabbath (Mark 3:1-6). Their rules were more important to them than a man's suffering. He was angry with the disciples when they tried to prevent little children from coming to him (Mark 10:13-16). He corrected them publicly. He was angry two times about the use of God's temple for profit rather than prayer. He made a whip, a mess, and a lot of noise. Anything that dishonored or misrepresented God angered Jesus.

If that is true, then abuse angers Jesus. Abuse is evil. It is sin. It damages the victim. It confuses people about the character of God. That means it angers Jesus. To be angry at abuse is good and right. Many of you are angry at your abuse and at the abuse of others. You are angry about having God misrepresented to you. You are angry because you have been told lies—about yourself and about God. Jesus is angry about those things too. He hates sin and its ability to destroy those he loves. He knows about anger.

At the same time, we need to keep in mind that anger is a fast-moving emotion. It rises up and out very quickly. It is very easy to just let our anger take over and impulsively act on it. We must remember that we are sinful people. We are self-centered. The Bible says, "Be . . . slow to become angry" (James 1:19). We are cautioned with good reason. Jesus' anger rose up out of a perfect heart. Ours rises up out of no such thing. Being angry in a right way requires a lot of work before God. It requires work that will continue for a lifetime.

Does Jesus know grief as well? He certainly does. He bore our griefs (Isa. 53:4, NASB). Jesus has carried all of the grief you have ever felt, all of the grief that every survivor has ever felt, all of the grief that every suffering human being has ever felt. I do not know how he stood it. Mark's gospel tells us that Jesus was overwhelmed with sorrow (Mark 14:34). To be overwhelmed is to feel as if you are drowning. It means you feel crushed, completely overcome in mind and feeling. It is too much. It is unbearable.

Jesus felt that too. On several occasions he groaned (Mark 7:34; John 11:33). A groan is a deep sound that expresses pain for which there are no words. Jesus grieved. He wept. Tears ran down his face. God openly cried. He didn't hide it. He didn't tough it out in public. He wept.

You who have felt such sorrow and grief can know that Jesus knows. Jesus has not only felt grief; he has *carried* yours. You who feel as if the tears will never stop have a Redeemer who has cried. He has groaned, been overwhelmed, been flattened by the crush of sorrow. He *knows*.

This Jesus we worship is not some pale, dispirited, passionless being. He not only felt what you feel, he felt it intensely. His emotions were an accurate representation of the heart of God.

Some of you, as the result of abuse, have become flat, passionless. You flee from your feelings. Others of you are imprisoned by your emotions. They ride you up and down and easily lead you to believe lies about yourself and God. Know with certainty that, although such feelings as grief and anger can be frightening, God does not want you to obliterate them. He felt them. We are called to be like him. Know also that he who has redeemed you is able to work redemptively with your emotions. They are not outside his power to heal and control. Let yourself dwell on the emotional suffering of the Redeemer, and let those meditations draw you close to him for understanding, for comfort, and for healing.

20

Healing for Your Thinking

In chapter 15 we considered how sexual abuse damaged your thinking. Let me remind you that there is hope. Healing *will* come for your thinking patterns. It will come through replacing the lies with truth. Healing will come through the power of the Redeemer. Listen first to the voices of these survivors:

> *"I am in my late forties, and I am slowly begin-*
> *ning to say what I think without apology. It is*
> *still a struggle. I still explain myself too much.*
> *I still have trouble letting my 'yes' be 'yes' and*
> *my 'no' be 'no.' After being silenced for so long,*
> *speaking my thoughts out loud, even thinking*
> *that they have value, is a new experience for me."*
>
> *"My thinking was so mixed up. I spent most of*
> *my life pretending not to remember what my dad*

had done to me. I pretended, to myself and to others, that I had the perfect family. When I was twenty-five, I let myself think and then speak what was true. It has changed me and my life irrevocably."

"I am learning, by continual practice, to tell the truth from lies. I used not to see the lies at all. Then I could see them with help. Now, when a lie goes through my head, I will often find myself recognizing it for what it is and saying, 'Wait a minute, that's not right. What is true here, and what is not?' It is like using muscles for the first time. When they are atrophied and you try to do something with them, they don't work so well. Over time they get stronger and stronger."

THE JOURNEY TOWARD HEALING

If you have been sexually abused, your thinking has been shaped by the abuse. That's not a nice thought. All of our thinking has been shaped by the experiences and people in our lives. Unfortunately, abuse is no exception. Not only that, but the thoughts we acquire in intense moments tend to get burned more deeply into our brains. If you were chronically abused, then that "burning into your brain" happened over and over.

For example, consider a six-year-old girl who is repeatedly raped by an adult male who tells her things such as: "God told me to do this," and "God has daddies teach their little girls this way," and "If you weren't such a whore, I wouldn't have to do this," and "You are nothing but trash." How many times do you suppose such a thing has to happen for that little girl to be sure those things are true?

Then, when the six-year-old goes to Sunday school, she hears that God loves her, that he will protect her, and that parents love children. In the end, what beliefs will control this young girl's thinking—the Sunday school teaching or the messages she hears from her abuser while he is raping her? The impact of the abuser and the abuse will control the girl's thinking. Abuse, in this case, becomes the overriding experience. The girl may believe that God is strong, but she believes her daddy is stronger. She may believe that Jesus loves little children, but he certainly couldn't love her. These control' beliefs become the basis by which all other information is processed.

It is important to note that this dynamic can occur as a result of "only" one rape. The reason for that is that trauma can shatter an entire worldview in less time than it takes for the trauma to occur. Most of us do not walk around with a worldview that allows for us to be raped at any moment. We couldn't tolerate the anxiety provoked by such a belief. We comfort ourselves with thoughts that assume tomorrow will be the same as today, or if I do it right, it will turn out okay. That is why when anything sudden and bad happens (such as a car accident), we often think almost immediately, "This can't be happening to me!" Why not? Is the world so nice that such things don't happen? Are we so special that we expect to be exempt from bad things?

When a bad thing happens, we have to find a way to adapt our thinking to accommodate the new information it has brought. We discussed in chapter 15 some of the ways we might use—doublethink, dissociation. In other words, we somehow split in our minds. We put the bad thing over in a corner by itself so that we can continue to think whatever we believed before it occurred. The problem with that is two-fold. First, such a mechanism does not usually work forever. Somewhere down the road, whatever got stuck in the corner rises up and demands attention. Second, and more important, to live split is to fail to live in truth.

Probably most of you who are reading this book have been abused in some fashion. What do you know to be true about life? There are evil people out there. The world is full of lies and deceit. People will do terrible violence to others to gratify something twisted in themselves. There is darkness, chaos, and trash out there. Sorrow can be crushing. Grief can be unremitting. Rage can be uncontrollable. Fear can overwhelm. I am not in control. I cannot always protect myself or those I love. I will not always get what I need. I am capable of hurting others. I am capable of lies and deceit. It makes you want to live a really long time, doesn't it? Right.

Some of you also know that beauty exists. You believe in love, and you have seen it in action. You have known people to speak truth even when it cost them. You have had a glimmer of the light that is there. Some of you want only these good things to be true, so you pretend that the bad things don't exist. Some of you have lived so long in the bad things that you can't find beauty and have never felt love.

How are we to live with these realities? How do we do that without doublethink or pretense or denial? How do we do that and stay sane? To be sane means to live in accord with reality, with truth. Good and evil are both realities; they are both true. Many of us live out of only one or the other.

The New Testament gives us a way to look at our

dilemma: "We know that we are children of God, and that the whole world is under the control of the evil one. We know also that the Son of God has come and has given us understanding, so that we may know him who is true" (1 John 5:19-20). This verse clearly states the tension with which we live. We are told here that those who have come to know and love Christ are the children of God. We are also told that God's children live in a very dangerous world. This is evidenced in Jesus' prayer for us that we would be protected from the evil one (John 17:15). Scripture assures us that the evil one ultimately cannot harm us, even though for now we live in a world that lies in his grip. Jesus himself calls our enemy "the ruler of this world" (John 14:30, NASB). The evil one lusts for power and will gratify those lusts at any expense. He is the destroyer, the life killer. He is the father of lies and the master of deceit. He is the accuser and the stalker of the children of God. Remember what we said in our peek behind the scenes in chapter 12?

The 1 John passage explains the world we live in, doesn't it? It doesn't mince words or soften the blow. It makes the world sound like an awful place to live. It makes things like sexual abuse, violence, perversion, and deception seem like logical conclusions of the evil one's control. If the whole world lies in the power of the evil one, then, of course, these things happen. There is truth here. It is truth we want to avoid. We would rather make it pretty. We want God to stop it from being a reality. It is, however, true.

But it is not the *whole* truth.

The passage also says, "We know *also* that the Son of God has come" (emphasis added). And not only has Christ come, but he tells us that the ruler of this world has no authority over him. This passing world order and its ruler are on their way out. The power of the evil one will be brought to an end. In the meantime, as we wait, groaning with all of creation (Rom. 8:22), the world is indeed messed up, and abuse hurts like crazy. *But* we know also that the Life Giver has come. We know also that the Healer has come. He is the Lover of Souls, the Burden Bearer. We know that the Comforter has come. Not only has he come, but we are told that he has "given us understanding, so that we may know him who is true." We are *not* given understanding so that we can perfectly figure out God or the mystery of why this world suffers. We *are* given understanding so that we may know him. And as we know more and more of him, he works to transform us into *his* image, beginning *in* us the work that will someday be evident in all things.

Because of the evil one, you need healing. God has made a way for you to know the Healer. Because of the evil one, you need love. God has made a way for you to know the Lover of Souls. Because of the evil one, you need someone to help carry your terrible grief. God has made a way for you to know the Burden Bearer. Because of the evil one, you need comfort. God has made a way for you to know the Comforter.

Stop a minute and make two lists in your notebook. First, what are the truths you know that fit with God's truth that this world is in the power of the evil one? Second, what are the truths you know about the Son of God who has come? Do not write what you think you should write. Write what you *know*. Some of you may have many things on your first list but may not be able to write anything on the second list other than the fact that the Son of God has come. This is not a theology test. Simply speak truth about what *you* know.

THE VOICE OF THE REDEEMER

Our Redeemer has not only inhabited a body like ours and felt emotions like ours, he has also been at the center of the battle between lies and truth. He who is truth waged war with the father of lies. He knows what it means to fight lies and deceit. He knows the strength of some of those lies. He fought against the liar himself so that you might have hope of living in truth.

You live in a world where you have encountered evil people. So did he. Some of you have known violence because of others' twisted need to gratify themselves. So did he. He, too, has encountered darkness, chaos, and trash. He went to hell—the place of greatest darkness and chaos. He who is sovereign over all knows what it is like to have hideous things happen and not be in control. He who is our refuge knows what it is like to be unprotected, not only from the fury of the enemy but also from the wrath of God. He knows what it is like not to get what you need. He had no place to sleep. He who created food and water went hungry and thirsty.

Why do I keep pointing you to the experience of the Son of God? You see, I cannot explain the mystery of suffering to you. I have no satisfactory answer as to why God allows abuse. I do not know why some children are allowed to suffer so deeply with not one human to help. I do not know why God does not stop it. I will not pretend to have such answers for questions I know you ask and struggle with fiercely. I do, however, know the character of God. That character has been revealed in Jesus Christ. God came and put on a body like yours, walked this world while it was in the power of the evil one, and was subjected to all of its horrors. He has felt what you feel and then some. He has struggled with lies. He has endured unimaginable pain. He *knows*. He was made like us so that he can serve us mercifully and faithfully (Heb. 2:17). He was made like us so that when we speak to him of things no one else understands, he will know. You are understood. You make sense to him. It is he who can help you untangle the lies from the truth.

Listen to the words of a survivor as she reflects on the process of therapy, her struggle to give voice to her life, and her war with the lies that resulted: "There is a mystery to being heard. Speaking horrible secrets out into the light of day kills off a lot of their power. When you take a lie from the pit and put it up against the truth of Christ, you see it for all its evil and bullishness. Tell a child over and over that she is not worth protecting, and she not only believes it, she lives it. Years later, be brave enough to struggle with her and show her that she is so important that God was willing to die for her. Suddenly those lies begin to fall at the feet of the cross. It may still hurt sometimes. It may still haunt sometimes, but she does not live with it in the same way. Her pain no longer comes from believing the lie. Rather, there is pain about how and when the lies were made, pain over those who made them, and pain that there are any lies at all. It is a very different struggle. It is a struggle with living rather than with dying. It is a good place to start."

There is a Redeemer. He is truth, and the truth will set you free.

21

Healing for
Your Relationships

I n chapter 16 we considered how sexual abuse damaged
your relationships. Let me remind you that there is hope.
Healing *will* come for your relationships. It will come as
you are set free from your fears and enabled to move out in
love. Healing will come through the power of the Redeemer.
Listen first to the voices of these survivors:

> *"Broken trust has affected my life so deeply and
> completely that I do not think I will be totally
> healed in this area apart from being in heaven
> with Jesus. However, I am growing and trusting
> more. As a matter of fact, I never thought I
> would be able to trust as much as I do now. So
> who knows how much I'll grow?"*

> *"I am learning not to demand that others be for
> me what they cannot be. I was so needy and had*

such high expectations. It was humanly impossible for people to be what I wanted them to be. I am learning to recognize others' limitations as well as my own. I am asking God to transform my thinking about relationships daily. I am slowly learning something of his grace when dealing with others."

"One of the most freeing truths for me relationally has been something my therapist taught me. When I do not like what is happening in a relationship, I can first of all speak truth in a loving way. Lots of times nothing happens. I used to panic and start to push and pull on the other person. I am learning to trust the work of God's Spirit in that person instead. He will move in each of our lives and be the one to bring about change."

THE JOURNEY TOWARD HEALING

We spoke in chapter 16 about how abuse occurs in the context of relationship. The resulting lies and confusion spill out into other relationships. We may end up isolated while longing for intimacy. Trust is broken, and we guard our borders, vigilantly protecting ourselves from harm. Limits, our own and others', make little sense when they have been repeatedly ignored by others. We intrude, and others get angry or annoyed. We overcommit, not understanding that limits are normal and that it is okay to say no. We long for love yet erect a wall. We trust blindly. It gets overwhelming and complicated, and we want to give up.

It is important to understand that you cannot figure out relationships by yourself. We learn about relationships *in* relationships. We are supposed to learn about relationships while we grow up, ideally from our parents. We learn from our parents as they interact with us and as they teach us directly, "No, don't do that" or "That is a helpful response in that situation." We learn from them whatever they do. Unfortunately, they sometimes teach us all the wrong things.

One of the key components in healthy relationships is understanding what it is realistic to expect. When we grow up in a negative environment, we do one of two things. First, some of us expect nothing. We never open our mouths, express ourselves, or ask for anything. It doesn't even occur to us. Relationships mean figuring out what other people want and giving it to them so that we won't get hurt. If what we thought, wanted, or needed didn't matter for eighteen years, why would we assume the rest of the world would be any different? Sadly, many people will continue to take advantage of us and simply reinforce the lesson we learned. Second, others of us realize that what we are getting is all wrong. We try to figure out what life ought to be like. Our figuring gets mixed up with our longings, and the result is usually unrealistic expectations. For example, if you grew up in a home full of rage, you probably expect that in a home where people love each other, no anger at all will be expressed. Then when you see anger expressed, you panic, assuming that any anger means the collapse of love.

You cannot work out how to express yourself to others without being in relationship to others. You cannot learn realistic expectations for people without being in relationship to people. That means that in order to grow relationally, you will have to be in relationship. Scary, right?

How do you go about establishing relationships that are helpful when you don't even know what to look for? The two best places I know to do that initially are in a counseling relationship and in the church community. These are not perfect places; some evil people can be found in the counseling profession and in the church. But I believe that counseling and the church community are still the two best places. Chapters 23 and 24 will give guidelines for how to find a good counselor and for how people in the church community can effectively walk alongside you. I hope that those guidelines will enable you to be discerning, but they will not protect you from hurt.

No relationships are free from hurt. Not all hurt is abuse, and not all hurt leads to abuse. Learning to tell "normal" hurt from "abnormal" hurt is a difficult process. Learning how to respond when you are hurt in either way is also difficult. Learning to hang on to the truth that the wrongs of others are manifestations of their hearts, rather than a commentary on how awful you are, will take lots of repetition. Having the courage to look at yourself and your own heart instead of exclusively focusing on what others are doling out and how you might need to guard against them will take hard work.

You long to be known and loved by someone with skin on. That is normal. You were *made* to be in relationship. You long to speak and be heard. You long to matter. That, too, is what you were meant to do. The people with whom you will relate long for the same. It takes all of us a lifetime of learning and growing to do relationships in a way that is not destructive to ourselves or to others.

The Basis of Relationship

If you have been sexually abused, the basis of most of your
relationships is fear. That fear, which is the result of the
trauma of the abuse, has an impact on every one of your relationships. Fear produces caution, wariness, careful observation.
Fear results in self-protection. Such characteristics are not
all bad. We *should* be careful in our relationships. We *should*
observe others. And we *should* walk away from some situations. However, there is a tremendous difference when those
responses are the result of love rather than fear.

Fear guards; love welcomes. Fear hides; love pursues.
Fear shuts up; love expresses. Fear panics; love waits. Fear
keeps a record; love forgives graciously. To move out of fear
and into love is a tremendous shift. The apostle John tells us
that "there is no fear in love. But perfect love drives out fear,
because fear has to do with punishment. The one who fears
is not made perfect in love" (1 John 4:18).

People sometimes have the mistaken notion that acting
out of love toward someone means simply doing whatever
that person wants. That is not what love looks like. If I relate
to you out of fear, I will do things that will protect me from
what I fear. If I relate to you out of love, I will not simply be
putting aside what I want for what you want. You may want
some very wrong things. I am not to exchange being governed
by my selfish nature for being governed by your selfish nature.
Rather, if I relate to you out of love, then what I do will be
governed by the love of God, and the love of God will probably call me to do some very hard things! His love may call
me to let go of things I prefer to protect. It may require me to
speak to you truth that I prefer not to speak. One thing I do
know: God's love will continually call me to do things that do

not come naturally to me. It will expose my heart. I will find that often when I appear most loving to the observer, I am, in fact, simply serving my own ends, protecting my reputation, soliciting points. I will also find that when an observer may judge my actions to be unloving, I may be doing something extremely difficult, something that was done out of sheer obedience to God.

The verse quoted previously says that "fear has to do with punishment." Fear does indeed cause us to punish others. We punish when we seek revenge because someone has done what we were afraid they would do. We punish when we hate. We punish when we withhold or withdraw. We punish when we fail to speak truth. We punish whenever we do not act in love.

Fear also torments. I live in fear that you will hurt me. I fear you will not give me enough—enough attention, enough adoration, enough love. Fear drives me to measure constantly. Fear torments me to make sure I am hiding adequately. Fear torments me to wonder if you will discover and then reject the real me. Fear is never at rest.

In the previous chapters we have spoken a great deal about truth and lies. We have talked about the darkness and confusion that result from lies. We have talked about the freedom that truth brings. I know that you long for truth and light and freedom. In reading a New Testament passage, I learned something startling about how we see clearly. "Whoever loves his brother lives in the light, and there is nothing in him to make him stumble. But whoever hates his brother is in the darkness and walks around in the darkness; he does not know where he is going, because the darkness has blinded him" (1 John 2:10-11).

According to this Scripture passage, if we want to see clearly, we must love. Wherever we do not love, we cannot see clearly. The Greek word for *hate* in this verse literally means "to love less." That covers a lot of ground. If we hate, resent, or fear another, we invite darkness into our own lives! We will be blind, and we will stumble. That means that the very thing we hope our fear will result in—self-protection—is the very thing that will be destroyed. We are hardly safe if we are walking in darkness and stumbling.

Now, I know this touches on huge and volatile issues such as forgiveness. It brings up long-buried feelings, feelings that run deep. I know that any talk of forgiveness and loving when you have been sexually abused and are left with the litter of that experience all over your life results in strong reactions. Listen to these survivors:

> *"I have carried wounds inflicted by people who used me in an effort to meet their own needs illegitimately. I have done the same thing every time I have sought to control a relationship in order to gain affirmation for myself. I have been out recruiting my own circle of 'need meeters.' Even when my approach was to be the helper, it was still an effort to take care of me. I began to recognize that I, too, used other human beings for my own purposes. The recognition that I abused people too was so sickening after my own experience of being abused that it drove me back to the cross in a more profound way than I have ever experienced before. Jesus' power to heal my wounds is greater than I ever thought. To my*

*surprise, it isn't nearly as dear to me as his
power to forgive my sins. There is redemption."*

*"I was filled with hate. I rationalized my
attitude by believing that although God offers
us forgiveness, we also have to ask for it. Since
no one was asking for my forgiveness, I did
not have to give it. God's Word is undeniable.
Slowly I began to see my sin. Time after time,
Jesus teaches us to love our enemies and offer
forgiveness unconditionally. I do not believe that
my family deserves forgiveness, but that is not
the point. I longed to be free from the bitterness
and rage that were destroying me. Slowly, I
began to open myself up to the possibility of
forgiveness, and my life began to change. God
softened my heart and filled me with love. It
was like opening the windows on a beautiful
spring day. I believe that forgiveness is part
of the healing process and is itself a process.
Forgiveness has little to do with your abuser.
Forgiveness is about freedom from destructive
thoughts and emotions. Forgiveness is about
fellowship with God."*

THE VOICE OF THE REDEEMER

We discussed in previous chapters that Jesus inhabited a
body, felt emotion, and faced lies. Jesus also lived in relationship with people. He also lived in relationship with God.
What were relationships like for the One who was perfect
love?

Think of some of the major components of your abuse in a relational sense. Words like *rejection, betrayal, ridicule, silent witness,* and *abandonment* come to mind. Those words describe terrifying, gut-wrenching experiences. To live through one of them is to live through something awful. Abuse often includes them all, and then some.

Did Jesus experience rejection? The religious leaders of the day certainly rejected him. They said he was possessed by the devil or had an unclean spirit (Mark 3:20-30). They tried and found guilty the only guiltless person to walk this earth. He was misrepresented and given no credibility. The people who had followed him turned around and, incited by the leaders, tossed him out to die. The Redeemer was rejected by his disciples. The men whom he loved and taught eventually ran off in fear.

Did Jesus experience betrayal? He was certainly betrayed by Judas, who had been in his inner circle. The Redeemer was betrayed by the crowds who had been personally touched by many of his miracles.

Jesus knew ridicule. He was scorned, despised, and tormented. His words were not considered credible. Many stood by, knowing he did not deserve death; they served as silent witnesses. They turned a blind eye and let it happen. The Redeemer was abandoned by all.

Perhaps most staggering is that the Father—whom Jesus loved and served perfectly—abandoned him, rejected him, and was silent as he died. That is the darkest place that ever existed in a relational sense. The Redeemer knows utter aloneness.

Who betrayed you? Your father? your mother? your uncle, grandparent, brother, or teacher? Jesus knows the sting of that. By whom have you been rejected? Some of you have experienced rejection by many people: your abuser, your peers, your churches, your spouses. Jesus knows the aloneness of that. Some of you have been abandoned by those who should have stood by you. Someone silently watched your abuse and did nothing. Jesus knows the darkness of that. Many of you were ridiculed. You were used sexually and then made fun of for not "doing it right." You were criticized, berated, verbally tormented. Your Redeemer knows the humiliation of that.

Relational pain is a deep kind of pain. It is not a superficial wound. Jesus knows the depth of your pain. He calls to you to give him all of the pain and all of the hurts because he cares for you (1 Pet. 5:7).

There is a Redeemer. He heals wounds, frees prisoners, forgives sin, and understands pain.

22

Healing for Your Spirit

I n chapter 17 we considered how sexual abuse damaged your spirit. Let me remind you that there is hope. Healing *will* come for your spirit. It will come through learning the character of God as it is revealed in Christ Jesus. Healing will come through the power of the Redeemer. Listen first as these voices describe what he experienced:

> *"He was despised and rejected by men, a man of sorrows, and familiar with suffering. Like one from whom men hid their faces he was despised, and we esteemed him not." (Isa. 53:3)*

> *"Look to my right and see; no one is concerned for me. I have no refuge; no one cares for my life." (Ps. 142:4)*

> *"Scorn has broken my heart and has left me helpless; I looked for sympathy, but there was*

*none, for comforters, but I found none."
(Ps. 69:20)*

*"The cords of death entangled me, the anguish
of the grave came upon me; I was overcome by
trouble and sorrow." (Ps. 116:3)*

"A band of evil men has encircled me. . . . People stare and gloat over me." (Ps. 22:16-17)

*"The wicked man hunts down the weak. . . . He
is haughty. . . . He lies in wait . . . watching
in secret for his victims. . . . He lies in wait to
catch the helpless. . . . His victims are crushed,
they collapse; they fall under his strength. He
says to himself, 'God has forgotten; he covers his
face and never sees.' " (Ps. 10:2, 5, 8-11)*

*"My God, my God, why have you forsaken me?
Why are you so far from saving me, so far from
the words of my groaning?" (Ps. 22:1)*

*"In bringing many sons {and daughters} to
glory, it was fitting that God, for whom and
through whom everything exists, should make
the author of their salvation perfect through
suffering." (Heb. 2:10)*

THE JOURNEY TOWARD HEALING

I know that many of you struggle hard in your relationship
with God. Some of you fear him. Many of you do not trust him.
Some of you feel too dirty to come to him. Others have given up
hope of any relationship with him. You fear it, don't want it, or
are sure he doesn't love you anyway, so what does it matter.

I also know you struggle hard with questions about your life and yourself. Why me? Why anybody? God could stop it; why doesn't he? How can I trust the One who let it happen? How do I know he won't let it happen again? What kind of God is he? Why would he want me? And if he does want me, then what do I have to do to keep being wanted?

I have already confessed that I cannot answer such questions. I cannot give answers that will result in your feeling satisfied. I don't know anybody who can. I cannot answer the whys. I can only tell you *who*.

We work hard as human beings to understand things. We want to understand weather patterns, machines, and other people. We want to understand ourselves. We are often driven to explain why this disaster happened, why this machine is good, why someone else hurt us, or why we did something a certain way. It is not bad to want to understand. God gave us minds that work like that. Many wonderful things have occurred in this world because of our ability and drive to understand.

The problem is not that we want to understand. The problem is that we cannot understand everything. Our minds are finite, limited. That means that there are things I will never understand. Some of my limitation is simply due to the particular mind that I have. It is *not* a machine mind! (Any number of friends will attest to that!) Some of my limitation is due to lack of study. I am perfectly capable of grasping some subject areas if I would just put the time in to do so. (Who knows, maybe I could even understand machines!) Some of my limitation is due to my finiteness. It doesn't matter how much I study or even how good my mind is; there are things I cannot comprehend. I am a little person, in a massive universe, with a finite brain. God, in his totality, will simply not fit in my brain.

The result of all of this is that I will not understand many things about God. And guess who decides what most of those things are? Not me! God has revealed to us what he wants us to know. There are many things he has not explained. The why of suffering is one of them.

My father suffered from a debilitating illness for over thirty years of his life. That fact has influenced me in life-altering ways. To this day, I cannot tell you why my father suffered. I can tell you what I have learned about myself and others because of his suffering. I can tell you how that has influenced my work with the suffering of others. I can tell you that I have learned many things about God as a result of that experience. But I cannot tell you why it occurred.

Tucked away in a prophecy in Isaiah is this beautiful promise from the Lord: "I will give you the treasures of darkness, riches stored in secret places, so that you may know that I am the Lord . . . who [calls] you by name" (Isa. 45:3). This world can be a very dark place. You have lived in places of darkness. You know the pain and heaviness of those places. You do not understand why you went there. You did not want it, and you do not want what it has done to you.

I cannot explain to you the ways of God. I *can* tell you of the character of God, and it is there that you will find the treasures that are hidden in your darkness. It is hard to change the question. We start with why. That is understandable. It is difficult to change from "Why did it happen?" to "Who are you?" One of the reasons is that we assume that *what* happens to us teaches us the truth about *who* God is. It does not. We live in a world that lies in the power of the evil one, and everything he does is riddled with lies. Lies that are calculated to have us believe that God is not good but evil. If we mindlessly allow circumstances to tell us who God is, then we will believe abominable things about him. Many do.

It is my hope and prayer that one of the results of reading this book will be a longing in you to know God as he is revealed in Jesus Christ. Jesus, we are told in John 1:18, has explained the Father to us. If you want to know who God is, then study Jesus. The quotations at the beginning of this chapter are about this Jesus. He is "fit" to be your Savior because he, too, has suffered from the darkness.

When we are in pain and go to share with people, we want and need them to understand. We need them to "get it." And we need to know that they do. A person who does not understand our suffering is not fit to come alongside. Many of you have had unfit people try to help you. What happened? They hurt you more. Jesus is fit, perfect. Why? Because he suffered.

The treasure in the darkness is Christ. You will not find him over with the pretty people. He was not one of them. You will not find him with the appreciated, sheltered, admired people. He was not one of them. You will find him with the rejected, betrayed, abandoned, abused, and ridiculed people. You will find him with the filthy, demonized, outcast people. And when you find him in the dark and secret places, places you have wanted to excise out of your life, you will find that he *knows*. And not only does he know, but he knows so well that he calls you by name.

THE VOICE OF THE REDEEMER

How do you begin to find Jesus? You will find him in his Word. You will find in the Bible much that will relate to your suffering, to the abuse, to the feelings that resulted, and to who Jesus is. Study Psalm 10, where David is struggling with abusers. Look at Psalm 22, where you will find things about Jesus' experience. Keep asking the question "Who is he?" Go to Psalm 86, where David battles internally with the evil men around him and his desire to seek after God. Study Psalm 88, which closes with "the darkness is my closest friend." Isaiah 53 will bring the suffering of your "fit" Savior into bold relief. Study the Gospels, looking to understand Jesus' experiences as they relate to the areas we have considered—his body, his emotions, lies and truth, his relationships, and his walk with his Father.

Often, when working with survivors in these areas, I will encourage them to grapple hard with the Scriptures. One of the ways to do that is to write in your notebook as you read. The minute something strikes you, stop. We tend to read to the end of a chapter, as if somehow that were the right thing to do. It is far better to stop and wrestle with one phrase than to keep going for the sake of finishing something. We often fail to heed the voice and work of the Spirit when we just plow ahead.

Turn what you read into a prayer. Use the words of Scripture to help you articulate your pain, your questions, your fear, your anger. Record those prayers in your notebook.

Rewrite the Scripture passages you read. Personalize them. Take Isaiah 53, and write it so it speaks about your life. Then look hard at the similarities in your life and the life of Jesus. Does he know?

Listen to the voice of this survivor (whom I will call Jessica), who personalized parts of Isaiah 53, writing as if Christ were speaking:

"There wasn't anything about me or going for me that would make someone want me or want to be with me, much less listen to me. I was not beautiful. My body was of an ugly form. People would turn away from me. I wore remade clothes. I was poor. I was laughed at by my peers and shunned by those older than myself.

"I was despised. Kids around me rejected me. I know what it means to be hurt. I know what it means to have the heart so filled with pain that it seems you can endure no more, yet it continues. I know what it is like to have people turn and look the other way. I know what it is to have a life of sorrow and pain. I know what it is like—I know what it means to suffer, and suffer to the point of knowing that not only I am all alone—no one is with me who cares— but also that I will die. There is no one else to go to, and no one will listen. No one heard my cry for help and removed the hurt and pain that tears my insides apart and that makes me not care about my outside self either.

"I know. I know because my father allowed such evil to happen in my life that I would understand you better, Jessica. He said he loved me, but how could he when he allowed such awful things to happen to me? He allowed others to tear me to pieces, to whip my back, and to humiliate me. I was cut till my skin would bleed. I was crushed under the wrongdoing of other men. I was spat upon. I was cursed for who I was and was held responsible for all the things that happened. The punishment that others deserved fell on me. I was the one crushed, bruised, hurt. My heart was broken. My will to live died. My ability to see things clearly disappeared. But I had to live. I had to remain stable. I had to stand firm. I had to be someone. I went through everything— every imaginable thing there was. I suffered everything that you have suffered or will ever have to suffer. I know just what it is all about. I know what it means. I know the hurts in the deepest part of your heart. I know the pain of having nails being pounded into my body.

"I know intensely and personally the rejection of those you love. I was hung on a cross, and it was only minutes until I would die. There was no question in my mind that God had turned his back on me. He forgot about me. He left me alone. He could have changed things around. They could have been different. I needed him. I called to him. But instead he left me to die. He forgot about me. He left me alone. At a time when I needed him the most, he turned around and looked the other way.

"Now listen to me, Jessica. I was hurt so that you would be able to come to me with your hurts. I was despised so that you could come to me when someone turns and hates you. I was abused so that I would understand you. I was abused so that I could love you. I

was scourged so that I know what it was like
to be beaten. I had stakes pounded into my
hands and feet and my side split open. I had
a wreath of thorns that tore into my head. I
knew you would have to go through what you
did. I knew what it would mean. But I was
there for you in a very special way. I went that
route before you. You unfortunately had to
follow in some of the same steps I had to step
in. But I was there, and because of the pain
and destruction that would be done to you,
that is exactly why my life was as it was.

"You may have given up, and I can't blame
you. I would too. I knew the ultimate end of
my situation—you don't. You don't have even
the slightest idea of what is ahead of you in your
life. You've run from me for almost two years.
You're my little sheep. My little child. You've
gone your way. I've been distressed for you. I
suffered on the cross for you. I did not open my
mouth to have it taken away because I knew you
were forced to keep silent for so many years, and
if I would have pleaded for mercy, I would have
no answers to give to you. I was silent for you.
God caused this to happen. I didn't understand,
and it came to the point where I pleaded with
God while I hung on the cross—why, why have
you forsaken me? God's answer to me was this:
'You must do this for Jessica.'

"I was cut off from everyone. It was God's
will for me to be crushed and caused to suffer.

It was done for you and many others, but especially for you.

"Jessica, after it is all over, there will be light—a new path for you—and you will be satisfied. By knowing me, you will be able to help many."*

What are your thoughts after reading this? Take some time to write them in your notebook. Allow the personalization of this passage to remind you that *Jesus knows.*

The God we worship speaks. He has voice. He has expressed himself to us. We desperately need to listen. He also gave you voice. He longs for you to speak to him, and to speak honestly. Use these suggestions to help you interact with him. Listen to him. Speak to him. He *will* speak to you. He will show you the "treasures of darkness."

Hear the voices of these survivors who have found treasure in the darkness:

My Heart Reached Up

My heart reached up
And found
    The throne of God.
I, the discarded one, the
Empty, forsaken one . . .

My heart reached out
And felt
    The clasp of God.
I, the rejected one, the
Untouched, leprous one . . .

*A variation of this paraphrase first appeared in Counseling Survivors of Sexual Abuse (Carol Stream, Ill.: Tyndale, 1997), 138–141.

My heart reached in
And knew
  The love of God,
I, the hated one, the
Much maligned, fearful one . . .

My heart turned 'round
And saw
  The heart of God.
I, the beloved one, the
Redeemed, joyful one . . .

Here am I, Lord.
  Send me.
—written by Lynn Brookside, April 1994

"I have come to see evil for what it is—ever
present, dreadful, and most difficult to under-
stand. However, through that dark cloud a
light has shone, and his name is Jesus! How
different he looks to me now. He is sad, sad
about the terrible things others did to me and
sad about the pain it brought into my life. He
weeps. He loves me. My blindness was so great.
I could not see that he loved me. He has helped
me see all the pain he suffered at the hands of
evil men. He understands my pain. He knows."

May you, too, come to find that "he knows." *He* is the treasure
in the darkness.

Part Five
Finding Others to Help

WHEN we suffer, we need others to walk alongside.
God has called us to care for one another and to
give special attention to those who are weaker
(1 Cor. 12). Any survivor who is facing the pain
of abuse and seeking healing and transformation is
in a "weaker" place.

If you are a survivor of sexual abuse, it is important not only to have someone who will walk with
you but also to have someone who will know what
you need and don't need. When people don't know
what to do, they feel awkward and can unknow-
ingly damage someone who is already hurt.

The purpose of this section is twofold: to assist
you in getting the help you need and to give guidelines for people who choose to walk alongside you
on your journey.

23

Finding a Good Counselor

Some of you will conclude that you would like to find a professional counselor to help you sort through your experience and to walk with you in your journey toward healing. How do you make that decision? Listen to the voices of these survivors as they describe their experience with counseling:

> *"Even though I had to walk down the driveway of the therapist's office, it seemed to be an extremely long and uphill climb. Just taking that first step of walking into the office seemed to highlight the extreme struggles inside of me. I had seen other counselors before and although there had been some helpful 'surface changes' in my life, my deep 'inside self' was still damaged and untouched."*

> *"I did not know what was wrong with me except that I knew I was in trouble and I*

thought it had something to do with my child-hood. My head was full of words that wanted to be spoken. I needed someone to listen. I could not take being alone in it anymore. But who? How could I find anyone? Whenever I heard about counselors, I would ask questions. I wanted to hear how they treated people. I finally found someone who was highly recommended by someone I trusted."

Suppose you have come to the conclusion that you need to see a counselor. You want to. You don't want to. You need to. You are afraid to. Okay, you'll at least try it. Now what? How do you go about finding one? How can you tell a good one from a not-so-good one? You need to "shop" for a good counselor. Talk to trusted people who are in counseling. Ask them what they like or don't like about their counselor.

Let me suggest four areas that you need to consider as you seek help. I will also offer questions that you can ask counselors as you look for one that would be suitable for you.

1. Training. If you are going to pay money for the service of counseling, you have the right to ask about what you are going to get. A cluster of degrees on a wall does not guarantee that the counselor who earned them is a good counselor. However, part of effective counseling is knowledge, and training provides a great deal of knowledge. Here are some questions you might ask a counselor whom you are considering: What degrees do you have? What areas are they in? What are your areas of expertise? Have you had specific training for dealing with sexual abuse? What kind of training? Are you licensed in any way? If you plan to use your medical insurance to help pay for the counseling fees, the counselor will need to have a license of some kind. Check with your insurance company to see what its requirements are.

Now, I would like to be clear that training is no guarantee that you will get what you need. Over the years I have interacted with many relatively untrained people (as far as academic standards go) whose work with survivors is wonderful. My graduate program, which I completed twenty-five years ago, taught me nothing about sexual abuse. Training is simply one of the factors to consider. You will have to decide how important that is to you.

2. Experience. Counselors can have five degrees and no experience working with survivors of sexual abuse. But if they are excellent counselors in general, straightforward about their lack of experience, and willing to learn from you (not just you from them), they may do a terrific job. I learned from my clients. They were wonderful teachers, and they continue to teach me.

If a counselor lacks experience or training, you could ask whether or not he or she is getting supervision from someone who does have expertise in sexual abuse. Good supervision will fill in many gaps and prevent many mistakes.

3. Gender. Are you more comfortable with women than with men? Feel free to request a particular gender. Women who were abused by men and men who were abused by women often prefer a counselor whose gender is opposite to their abuser's. Counseling is scary enough without having to deal with that. Something to consider—many survivors have found it important to begin treatment with someone who is not the gender of their abuser, but they then have found it very healing toward the end to work with someone who is.

4. Faith. A crucial area is the faith of the counselor. What therapists believe permeates who they are and what they do. Again, you should feel free to ask questions. Anyone who knows and loves Christ will welcome such questions. One note of caution. The concept of spirituality seems to be popular these days. I am finding that many people will speak of themselves as Christians or "people of faith" when, in fact, they do not know Christ. That means that even though people say they are Christians, do not assume they mean the same thing that you do.

If you live in more rural or isolated areas, you will have fewer options. If that is the case, do not assume that a counselor who is not a Christian has nothing to offer you. If the counselors available to you have good training and experience with survivors, they can help you with many things. You will need to sort out what you hear (although, frankly, I hope you would do that with a Christian as well!). They will obviously not be helpful when it comes to your struggles with God.

However, remember that Scripture tells us that life ultimately comes from the Spirit. So while you may learn and grow from a counseling relationship, redemption comes from God, not from therapy.

Some survivors wonder what they *can* expect from therapy. While therapy alone does not give life, it can provide a safe place, support, encouragement, and a constant reminder of truth. The following note, which a client wrote to her therapist, expressed the value of therapy in her healing process.

"For your endurance, time, love, listening, and sharing the truth, I want to say thanks for walking the talk. I am so grateful that God brought me to you, a person who loves Jesus above all else and seeks his face and then walks me to the place where he is waiting to heal and strengthen me."

A FEW SUGGESTIONS

Let me offer a few more suggestions for finding a good counselor:

1. If you need referrals for counselors, you could contact two reliable groups: Focus on the Family (800/232-6459) and the American Association of Christian Counselors (800/526-8673).
2. If you end up in a counseling relationship and then find warning bells going off, speak up. If you say you are uncomfortable with certain things (such as touch) and you are disregarded, then you are not in a safe place. Remember the woman who talked about the warning signs she ignored when she went to her pastor for help?
3. You should have some sense that you are respected and heard in the relationship. Questions should be answered honestly and not defensively.
4. Your work may be long and will certainly be hard. You will need a relationship where you are safe and where repetition occurs without impatience.

Listen to the voice of this survivor describe what her counselor provided for her:

"*Much like a child learning to read, she sat with me as I sounded out unspoken, private pain. These were words I was afraid to speak and afraid to have heard. She stayed with me as I struggled. I am sure there were weeks, maybe months, where she would wait to say something. I realized, early on, that she spoke purposefully. Looking back, I see how she considered how much I could take and measured out truth in small amounts.*

"*She gave me many gifts. She listened to me, waited for me, paid careful attention to her timing, to how and when she spoke. She taught me that I could have different feelings at the same time, that I was not crazy to feel so confused, that I was stuck because I had too much to deal with alone. She brought sense to my turmoil. She helped me see clearly. She was sad for me, calmed me, redirected my thinking, hoped for me, ached for me, and worked hard, very hard for me. She respected me. From our very first meeting she wanted to know what it had felt like to be me.*"

24

Suggestions for People Who Are
Walking alongside a Survivor

T his chapter is for those of you who have chosen to accompany another in his or her struggle against the effects and damage caused by sexual abuse of some kind. Such a journey will be life changing and life giving. What follows is a letter from a person who reflects on her experience of obeying God's call to walk alongside a survivor, to enter into the survivor's suffering, and to share the joy of the survivor's healing.

Dear Diane,

One morning I was reading about the day before Jesus would be betrayed. He spent his time loving his disciples by washing their feet. His love for them was not dependent on their performance. He tells us that our love for others should be the same. I knew he was speaking to me when I read, "Now that you know these things, you will be blessed if you do them." I have, indeed, been unspeakably blessed as I have walked along survivors of sexual abuse. God's ways are indeed paradoxical. What often looked like a sacrifice to others was my greatest joy.

Here are some of the basic and essential things I found I needed to be a helper to a survivor of sexual abuse:

1. It was essential to acknowledge my own inadequacies. Abuse is more ugly than I ever imagined, and the damage done to a life is really beyond comprehension. Abuse is from the pit of hell, and the havoc it causes is terrible. I cannot make it better. I do not know the "solution." I am called to be there and to love.

2. The healing process takes a very, very long time. It takes longer than I often thought it should. I need to learn how to persevere. I need to be prepared to stay with it, even when I am not 'wanted.' I must be inviting, available, affirming, but not pushy.

3. We are in a spiritual battle. I had to ask God to equip me for the fight. Behind abuse is an enemy of the soul, an enemy who spreads lies, tries to enslave, and desires destruction. We must stand against "the spiritual forces of evil" on the survivor's behalf. We are called to intercede. I learned not to expect the survivor to fight for herself. God called me to intercede on her behalf.

4. I needed faith in God. Perhaps the most needed gift God gives us is faith, not in ourselves, but in what he can do. My friend was unable to trust God. All hope had been stolen from her. She needed me to believe for her. God gave me assurance that he could redeem any situation. My friend needed to be told that every

day. Even though she was not able to believe it herself for a very long time, I know it made a difference that someone in her life "saw" healing in her future, when she saw only darkness.

5. I had to protect myself. One of the most difficult things for me was to learn how to enter into another's pain without being drowned by it. Because the despair was so deep, it was difficult not to let it engulf me. I kept returning to this truth: "Greater is he who is in you than he who is in the world."

One of the greatest joys of my heart has been to be a part of God's restoration of one of his children. It is a miracle to see God tenderly peel off the layers of hurt and pain so that he can reach to the deepest part of the soul and heal from the inside out.

GUIDELINES

If you choose to walk alongside a survivor in his or her journey, you can learn from others' experience. First, you have made a good start if you have read this book. I suggest that you read other books to increase your understanding of the effects of sexual abuse. I have included a reading list at the end of this book.

Second, I share with you some specific do's and don'ts that will not only help you know what to do but also keep you from making mistakes that might damage an already wounded person.

Do . . .

1. Recognize the honor a person gives you if he or she chooses to tell you that he or she was sexually abused. In telling you, the person is deciding that you are a safe person.

Never underestimate the courage it takes to say, "I was sexually abused," for the first time. To drag to the light what has been a well-kept secret for decades is terrifying.

2. Realize that the sexual abuse of a child has deep and enduring consequences. This is especially true when the abuser was a family member, the child was very young, and the abuse has been kept secret for a long time.

3. Be willing to witness great pain. You will see great pain, hard questions, and anger. Many of us are uncomfortable with such things and want to make them go away.

4. Be willing to believe the unbelievable. Sitting with an incest survivor brings you face-to-face with some of the most evil and twisted things human beings do to each other.

5. Examine your own attitudes before God. Coming alongside a survivor of sexual abuse forces you to face your own preconceptions about sexual abuse, pain, good and evil, justice and injustice, males and females.

6. Assist the survivor in seeking professional help. The consequences of sexual abuse are complex. Help him or her find someone who has expertise in this area.

7. Find others who will help you form a support network for the survivor. A group of safe, loving people is better for the survivor and for you.

8. If the survivor is married, help the spouse find support and assistance in understanding the issues.

9. If the survivor is single, he or she may need a place to stay at times. Being alone with tormenting memories and nightmares is frightening.

10. Understand that dealing with memories of trauma almost always results in nightmares. A survivor can go through months and months of night terrors. Having some-

one to call in the middle of the night from a support network or through a crisis hot line is helpful.

11. Find out whether the survivor has a drug or alcohol problem.

12. Take any suicide threat seriously. Notify the counselor or take the survivor to a medical facility if he or she is threatening suicide.

13. Remember that incest is a criminal act.

14. Understand that healing takes time. God has created us to live in time, and we heal in time. Healing from sexual abuse is not a quick process. It shatters many fundamental things. Our God is a God of redemption, but he usually works through people and over time. Be patient. Then be patient some more.

15. Be aware of your vocabulary, your timing, and your body language. When we sit with someone in great pain, words of hope and peace are often our first response. Don't rush in. Listen. Words of love and hope will begin to make sense only as they are fleshed out in a relationship with you. I prayed earnestly for a woman I was working with years ago, asking God to show her how much he loved her. His answer: "*You* show her. You want her to know how much I love her? Then you demonstrate that love to her."

16. Be prepared for repetition. The survivor will need to tell the story many times. Your reassurances, your faith, and your hope will need repetition. You will need to speak truth again and again. The lies are strong.

Don't . . .

1. Don't think that sexual abuse does not occur in seemingly "good" families. It happens in pastors' homes, choir directors' homes, and "upstanding citizens' " homes.

2. Don't minimize what happened. Saying "At least you weren't killed" does not help the survivor. All sexual abuse is serious, even if the abuse occurred only once or if it never went beyond fondling. All sexual abuse is a violation of God's law.

3. Don't imply that the survivor is to blame for the abuse. Nothing is justification for abuse.

4. Don't excuse the abuser. Whatever the abuser's problems, they are never a mandate for abuse.

5. Don't react with visible shock, horror, or disgust.

6. Don't be afraid of anger and grief. Such feelings will be intense. If there is no emotion with the telling, then the survivor is probably still denying the impact.

7. Don't simply tell the survivor that he or she must forgive and forget. To tell the survivor to forget is ludicrous. The truth needs to be faced before the survivor will even know what needs forgiving. Forgiveness is the work of the Spirit of God, not a switch we flip on. A survivor can ask God to teach him or her how to forgive the evil of abuse. No survivor can just produce forgiveness. It is supernatural to forgive.

8. Don't think the survivor simply wants attention. Sexual abuse is shattering. The survivor *needs* attention, and you are right to give it. Love the survivor. Then love some more. And when you run out of love, get on your knees and plead with God to fill you with more of his love so you can go and love some more.

GENERAL SUGGESTIONS FOR RESPONDING TO SUFFERING

When dealing with people who have suffered deeply, you can respond in several helpful ways:

1. Write notes of encouragement. Notes require no immediate response, and they can be read again and again.

2. Do not wait for someone who is suffering to call you. Suffering debilitates. Those who suffer usually cannot take the initiative.

3. Include the survivor in fun things. Fun can be a momentary distraction from pain and suffering.

4. Intercede faithfully. Much of the battle is fought in this arena.

5. Know that you do not have all the answers (neither do I!). Your presence in the midst of suffering is a great gift.

6. Take care of yourself. You cannot be effective if you burn out. We often respond to suffering with one of two extremes: we either protect ourselves to gain distance from the suffering, or we absorb it like a sponge and then collapse. Sexual abuse is evil. Violence is evil. We are finite. Know your limitations. This is one of the reasons a support network is wise.

7. Seek Christ, who is the only source of life. Nurture your relationship to him continually. He is the only one who can confront evil and death victoriously.

RESPONSES TO SOMEONE WHO HAS BEEN RAPED

Statistics suggest that one woman in ten will fall prey to a rapist at some time during life. (Even though males are also victims of rape, I write these suggestions for female rape victims.) *Rape* is a word that strikes terror in the heart of women. Fortunately, much change has occurred regarding attitudes toward women who have been raped. There are, however, damaging misconceptions that still exist (She asked for it. If she had not worn a short skirt . . .). Rape is a crime of violence and should be treated as such. The following list of do's and don'ts can help you help someone who has suffered rape.

Do . . .

1. Let her know that it is often better to have given in to her attacker than to have resisted him.

2. Assure her the rape was not her fault.

3. Encourage her to write down the details of what happened. She will find that easier to do immediately after the incident rather than later, when she is being questioned or pressured to remember.

4. Encourage her to report the crime, but remember that it is ultimately her decision to make.

5. Encourage her to go to the emergency room or police immediately if the rape has just occurred.

6. Go with her to report the attack or to the emergency room. It is very traumatizing to be examined immediately following a rape, especially by a male doctor.

7. Encourage her to seek professional help. Someone trained to deal with the aftereffects of rape will be able to help her sort through what happened.

Don't . . .

1. Don't evaluate the victim according to a preconceived stereotype of what kinds of women get raped.

2. Don't press for details of the attack.

3. Don't react with visible shock, horror, and disgust.

4. Don't accuse her of being partially to blame.

5. Don't discourage her from reporting the rape.

6. Don't criticize her for not resisting hard enough.

7. Don't urge her just to forgive her attacker and not report it.

8. Don't even hint that she might have been spared if she had asked God for help or done something differently.

Like the woman who wrote the letter, may your entrance into the fellowship of survivors' sufferings—and Christ's suffering—bring you untold blessing and joy. It has done so for me.

25

Some Final Thoughts

T he people in my office joke about a habit that I have. Someone will ask me a question about something, and I will give a response. Inevitably, I will come back later and say, "I had a thought. . . . " I think this chapter is a written expression of that habit. I have written the book and closed it up. But wait a minute—I had a thought. . . .

We discussed earlier the fact that you and I live in a world that lies in the power of the evil one. We said that is why we have such horrors as the sexual abuse of children and adults. I also know, practically speaking, that as a result of that evil, many of you have never had some of your basic human needs met. Life is riddled with injustice. Some people grow up in loving, stable homes; some do not. Some people experience chronic sexual abuse; others have never been touched inappropriately by anyone. Many of you have suffered greatly. Many of you continue to suffer. You long for relief, and it is hard to find.

Several years ago a survivor I was working with spoke about her struggles and the great pain that accompanied them. She longed for some respite. One of the things she expressed was a longing to "go home." She hastened to add that she had no idea what that meant, for she had never had a "home." The place she had grown up in was anything but a safe place. However, the concept of "going home" somehow articulated for her a powerful longing.

The word *home* conjures up many things for us. Whether or not we have known a true home, we associate the word with things like security, safety, love, respite, belonging. Every human heart resonates to these words. I believe that is because we were created to live in such a place. We were meant to live safely, securely, loved, and belonging. Those were characteristics of the relationship Adam and Eve had both with God and with each other. Then sin came, and Adam and Eve's "home" was blown up. People who have lost a home to disaster talk about the feelings that accompany such a loss. They become transient, with the sense that they belong nowhere. They feel anxious and insecure. Their sense of safety is destroyed.

I suspect most, if not all of you, can relate to such feelings. You know the feelings that come when it seems that your "home" has been blown up. For many of you that occurred with the first fondling or violation. Safety was shattered. Home was never the same again. For others, it occurred later in life. A rape later in life destroys your sense of safety in this world. Even when it happened on a street far away, you still feel unsafe in your own home. You cannot settle down. You check locks. You listen alertly. The feeling of being "at home" is gone.

Now, we often hear teaching regarding the fact that

heaven is home. We are told (and rightly so) that this world is not home but a place we are merely passing through. We do not really belong here, and we will not truly feel at home until we see Jesus. All of that is true according to Scripture. Does that mean that any sense of home in this world is an impossibility? Do we have to resign ourselves to the fact that some people get a taste of the real thing but others do not and that nothing can change that? I don't think so. I think Scripture teaches us something about having a home while we are here.

We said that the world lies in the power of the enemy. We also said that the Son of God has come. What does that have to do with home? Jesus said, "I will not leave you as orphans; I will come to you" (John 14:18). To be orphaned is to be bereft of parents and without a home. David says: "Though my father and mother forsake me, the Lord will receive me" (Ps. 27:10). Many of you have been forsaken. Some of you are literally orphaned. Others have parents, but they never functioned as such. Others have been forsaken by friends, church family, or spouses as you have struggled with the issues of your abuse. What does Jesus mean when he says he will not leave you as an orphan but rather will come to you?

Later in the John 14 passage Jesus says, regarding those who love him, "We will come to him and make our home with him" (John 14:23). He is referring here to the coming of the Holy Spirit to indwell the believer. The Holy Spirit is coming as a "homemaker."

How is the Holy Spirit making a home in you? To go home usually means to go to a place of comfort. The name Jesus gives to the Spirit is Comforter. One of the ways he comforts is by making a home in us and for us. How does he do that? Home is a place where we belong. We feel connected. We fit. We are welcomed. Many of you have had the experience of not belonging—in a school crowd, in a church group, in a neighborhood, or in your childhood home. It is a painful feeling not to belong. We feel shamed, humiliated, rejected, unworthy.

Jesus said, in speaking of the Comforter, "You know him, for he lives with you and will be in you" (John 14:17). Do you hear that if you are a child of God, then you are no longer alone? You have a home filled with a loving companion who is not only with you now but also will be with you forever. This is not a home you grow up and leave. This is a home that goes with you wherever you go. You have been chosen and welcomed into this home. You have been adopted by the Lover of Souls. You may have abusers who have trashed and used you, parents who never loved you, siblings who do not care about you, spouses who have walked out on you. The pain of such things is unspeakable, yes. But you also have a home. You belong. You are loved. You are not alone.

Home is also a place where we are protected. Many of you know what it means to be left unprotected. In fact, for some of you, home was the least protected place you knew. Home was not safe. It is a terrifying thing to have to go home and know that it is the most dangerous place for you.

When we protect people, we cover them or shield them from danger. We work to preserve their safety. We protect little children when we keep them from running into the street. We protect a battered wife when we get her to a place of safety. The Spirit, who has come to make his home with you, is your protector and defender.

If you have been abused, you have had the experience of not being protected. You felt frightened and found no place to run. It was an awful moment. No one came to help. You were left without refuge. Something dies inside when that happens. If you are a child of God, the Spirit who makes a home in you is your protector. Now, I can just hear some of you saying, "Right. And where was he when I was being abused? Some protector." He has not promised to protect us completely from the evil in this world. I have been very up front with the fact that I cannot answer why. What he will do is anything and everything to preserve you in Christ. He will protect the life of God in you. He is your refuge from anything that would take you away from God.

Home is also a place where we are nurtured or fed. Some of you have had the experience of going home tired at the end of a long day and being greeted by the smell of a good dinner cooking. Someone is present to feed you. Someone has taken care that you will get what you need. It is a wonderful feeling.

Some of you have not known home as a feeding place but rather as a place of great deprivation. Some of you came home to a locked door and perpetual silence. Some of you had to fend for yourselves in order to eat. Others were never fed a comforting touch. Your minds were neglected and ignored. Interaction, nurture, and care were absent.

Jesus said, "I am the bread of life" (John 6:35). He also said that the Spirit would take from him and give to you. He is a nurturing, feeding Spirit. Are you hungry? Hungry for love? He will take you to the Lover of Souls. Are you hungry to have your mind fed? He is the Spirit of truth. Are you weary? He will feed you with rest. He is the One who nurtures and feeds the life of God in us.

Finally, home is a place of training. Many survivors, particularly those who have suffered from chronic abuse, talk about feeling as if they don't know how to "do life," how to function relationally. Either they had no training, or they were taught mostly wrong things. They never had parents who carefully trained them. Rather, they had parents who simply reacted (often abusively) in the moment. They feel as if they have to guess what to do. It is a scary thing.

To train means to guide the growth of something, to work with a particular aim in mind. When we train a vine or a bush, we prune it so it will take a certain shape. Our trainer is the Holy Spirit. He has made a home in you and will teach and train you. He trains by helping us in our weaknesses (Rom. 8:26). He does not criticize or ridicule. He helps. He comes to aid us in our weaknesses. He does not stand back and point. He comes in close to help. He trains us by guiding us into truth (John 16:13). When you are confused, blind, or unable to understand, he will enable you to see truth. He reaches down in the midst of our weakness, our messiness, and our groanings and lovingly, purposefully works to conform us to the image of Christ.

The work of the Holy Spirit is a spiritual work. It is not initially a visible work. It is the work of the unseen Spirit in the unseen places of our hearts. We find it so hard to walk by faith and believe that he is working. He works from the inside out. We (and often others in our lives) would prefer that he start with the outside first. We hurt, and we make terrible mistakes. We are sure our lives are unredeemable. All the while our home maker is working. Think again about a line from the poem at the very beginning of this book—"He is always, steadily, there. Quietly, reconnecting."

In the midst of your suffering, in the midst of the destruction others have wrought, I hope you can hear that the Comforter has come. He is there for you and in you. In the midst of your loneliness, in the midst of your disconnection, I hope you can hear that the home maker has come. He is making a home for you and in you even now. May his work in you redeem what is lost, bring life to places of death, and conform you to the image of Jesus.

Suggested Reading

Dan Allender, *The Wounded Heart* (Colorado Springs, Colo.: NavPress, 1990) and *The Wounded Heart: A Companion Workbook* (Colorado Springs, Colo.: NavPress, 1992).

Lynn Heitritter and Jeanette Vought, *Helping Victims of Sexual Abuse* (Minneapolis: Bethany House Publishers, 1989).

Cynthia A. Kubetin and James Mallory, *Beyond the Darkness* (Dallas: Word, 1992) and Cynthia A. Kubetin and James Mallory, *Shelter from the Storm* (Nashville: LifeWay Press, 1995).

Diane Mandt Langberg, *Counseling Survivors of Sexual Abuse* (Carol Stream, Ill.: Tyndale House Publishers, 1997).

Arlys Norcross McDonald, *Repressed Memories: Can You Trust Them?* (Grand Rapids: Fleming H. Revell, 1995).

About the Author

DIANE LANGBERG, PH.D., has been a licensed psychologist in private practice for twenty-five years and is the director of a group practice in Jenkintown, Pennsylvania. She is a speaker at local and national conferences for clergy, women, couples, students, and professionals. Dr. Langberg writes the counselor column in *Today's Christian Woman* magazine and has also written for *Marriage Partnership* magazine, *Urban Mission Journal,* and *Christian Counseling Today*. Her books include *Counseling Survivors of Sexual Abuse* (Tyndale, 1997) and *Counsel for Pastors' Wives* (Zondervan, 1988). Diane and her husband, Ron, live in Pennsylvania with their two sons, Joshua and Daniel.

Ways to help —
  p 48 — "talking" someone out of flashback